THE ECONOMY OF THE KINGDOM

OVERTURES TO BIBLICAL THEOLOGY

The Land
by Walter Brueggemann

God and the Rhetoric of Sexuality
by Phyllis Trible

Israel in Exile
by Ralph W. Klein

The Ten Commandments and Human Rights
by Walter Harrelson

Sharing Possessions
by Luke T. Johnson

A Whirlpool of Torment
by James L. Crenshaw

Texts of Terror
by Phyllis Trible

The Suffering of God
by Terence E. Fretheim

Love of Enemies
by William Klassen

New Testament Hospitality
by John Koenig

The Tragic Vision and the Hebrew Tradition
by W. Lee Humphreys

Jesus, Liberation, and the Biblical Jubilee
by Sharon H. Ringe

From Darkness to Light
by Beverly Roberts Gaventa

The Mighty from Their Thrones
by J. P. M. Walsh, S.J.

Biblical Perspectives on Aging
by J. Gordon Harris

The Economy of the Kingdom
by Halvor Moxnes

Editors

Social Conflict and Economic Relations in Luke's Gospel

THE ECONOMY OF THE KINGDOM

HALVOR MOXNES

FORTRESS PRESS Philadelphia

Biblical quotations, unless otherwise noted, are from the Revised Standard Version of the Bible, copyright 1946, 1952, © 1971, 1973 by the Division of Christian Education of the National Council of the Churches of Christ in the U.S.A., and are used by permission.

Library of Congress Cataloging-in-Publication Data

Moxnes, Halvor.
The economy of the kingdom.

(Overtures to biblical theology)
Bibliography: p.
Includes index.
1. Bible. N.T. Luke—Criticism, interpretation, etc. 2. Sociology, Biblical. 3. Economics—Biblical teaching. 4. Palestine—Economic conditions. 5. Palestine—Social conditions. I. Title. II. Series.
BS2595.2.M69 1988 226′.406 88–45230
ISBN 0–8006–1548–4

3449D88 Printed in the United States of America 1–1548

To my parents
Jørunn and Leif Hvidsten

Contents

Editor's Foreword

When Overtures to Biblical Theology was inaugurated over a decade ago, a stated aim was to "reach beyond old conclusions, set categories, and conventional methods." *The Economy of the Kingdom* is a clear instance of a move beyond conventional methods of biblical exegesis. Building on recent studies of the social world of the New Testament and the access to this world offered by cultural and social anthropology, Halvor Moxnes guides us through the Gospel of Luke as pilgrims in a strange, but fascinating land.

Starting with the enigmatic description of the Pharisees in Luke 16:14, as "lovers of money," Moxnes shows that this often misunderstood and potentially anti-Semitic epithet must be seen against the backdrop of the social conflicts and economic relations of Luke's Gospel. Fundamental to his presentation is the recognition that in antiquity "the economy" is not a separate institution but is interwoven in the rich tapestry of social life, including relations of reciprocity in a village and structures of patronage among the ruling elite. A key motif throughout his study is "the moral economy of the peasant," described as the economic values of an underprivileged group, values which the Gospel of Luke affirms.

Moxnes integrates cultural and anthropological studies of diverse societies with traditional methods of literary and redaction criticism in an eminently clear and readable fashion. He offers a fine introduction not only to the social world of Luke, but to a method of entering this world, that should encourage general readers and specialists in other areas of biblical exegesis to adopt similar approaches. Both his way of reading texts and the bibliography offered make this work a fine introduction to an important new direction in biblical studies.

The Gospel of Luke emerges with an engaging freshness when read along with Moxnes's observations. Necessities of ordinary life such as food and clothing, events such as banquets, practices of almsgiving and hospitality, and seemingly archaic institutions such as "stewardship" come alive in his pages. Moving beyond a description of social *realia*, Moxnes takes us into the symbolic world behind events and practices, and here argues that Luke's polemical description of the Pharisees is not so much historical description as a challenge to any system built on restrictive structures of power. Christians who engage the Gospel of Luke today may well see themselves as "the lovers of money."

This Overture should also be set, as the author notes, in our contemporary "social world," with its great gaps between rich and poor and with its widespread economic challenges. The past decade has witnessed an explosion of studies on Luke's attitudes toward wealth and riches, already detailed in Luke T. Johnson's contribution to Overtures to Biblical Theology (*Sharing Possessions: Mandate and Symbol of Faith* [1981]). The present work offers a distinctive challenge by showing how different is the social context of Luke's statements on the rich and poor, and warns against facile application of powerful texts such as the woes on the rich and satisfied (Luke 6:24–26) or the parable of the rich man and Lazarus (16:19–31). At the same time, by unpacking the symbolic word and values of the Gospel of Luke it helps this Gospel address and confront the values and symbols that form the web of contemporary economic and social relations.

Halvor Moxnes is a professor at the Institute for Biblical Research of the University of Oslo. He earned his Dr.Theol. degree there and spent two years as a visiting research fellow at Yale University. He has published *Theology in Conflict: Studies in Paul's Understanding of God in Romans* (NovTSup 53 [Leiden: E.J. Brill, 1980]), and has been an active participant in meetings of the

Society of Biblical Literature and the Catholic Biblical Association of America. His work offers a fine example of the vital dialogue between European and North American scholarship.

John R. Donahue, S.J.

Preface

The goal of this study is to offer a picture of Palestinian society at the time of Jesus as it is portrayed in Luke's Gospel. Neither the historical Jesus nor the historical situation of Luke but the social world of the Gospel narrative is our focus of attention.

Luke addressed his Gospel to communities at his own time to tell the life of Jesus (1:1–4) and to exhort and to give advice about Christian life. His readers were not confronted, however, with individual dogmatic statements or moral exhortations. Rather, they were drawn into the narrative world of the Gospel and almost became part of the stories about Jesus and his followers and opponents. As readers of Luke's Gospel today we can share the same experience. In order to "enter" Luke's narrative, however, we need to know more about the way in which he structures his picture of Palestinian society at the time of Jesus.

In order to grasp Luke's meaning, we have to approach his narrative in much the same way as we enter a foreign country. Much is familiar to us, but we soon realize that there are many subtle differences in the ways in which that society functions. Things that look familiar may have a different meaning, and we start asking questions: What are the norms and values of this society? What are the rules for social relations and human interaction?

These are also the kinds of questions that we shall address to Luke's Gospel. Luke does not give mere facts about Palestine at the time of Jesus; he gives meaning to this world and structures it according to his moral and social understanding. And it is of this understanding that we will try to sketch a clear picture. In particular, this study focuses on an often neglected aspect, the moral understanding of social relations and economic interaction. Issues like "rich and poor" and "almsgiving" are central to Luke's Gospel. Our goal is to see these issues, too, not as individual sayings, but as parts of Luke's universe. The title of this book, *The Economy of the Kingdom,* indicates the context within which Luke's position on economic interaction gives meaning.

Our entry point into Luke's world of social and economic relations is his description of the Pharisees, and more specifically, his accusation in 16:14 that they were "lovers of money." This is just one of a series of negative statements about the Pharisees that cause a serious problem of interpretation. Many recent dialogues between Jews and Christians have been concerned to correct the negative portrayal that the New Testament in general and the Gospels in particular have projected of the Pharisees. All too often polemical statements have been taken by Christians at face value, as historical facts. Most often the religious attitudes of the Pharisees have been vilified, but the accusation that the Pharisees were "lovers of money" also fits well into a long history of accusations against Jews for greed and avarice (remember Shakespeare's Shylock!).

On the basis of Jewish as well as Hellenistic traditional polemics it can be shown, however, that this statement is not to be taken as a historical fact. Therefore, it cannot be discussed as a question pertaining to the historical Pharisees in first-century Palestine. But this accusation does have a function within Luke's picture of the Pharisees and social relations in Palestine. The historical question turns into a question of meaning in a social context: How did Luke construe the social and economic interaction in which the Pharisees were engaged? To answer that question, the study attempts, by drawing on ancient economics as well as social anthropology, to develop a model of interaction that would be plausible to Luke and his community.

This aspect of the study has a bearing upon the larger issue of attitudes toward possessions, wealth, and poverty within Luke's society. The models for economic exchange and patron–client relationships descriptive of Luke's world are helpful for a better understanding of Luke's sayings about "poor" and "rich," about "alms," "selling" and "giving," and so forth, so that we do not read them within the framework of our present-day economic system.

After two initial chapters that state the questions to be addressed and offer an overview of the Pharisees within the literary structure of Luke's writing, chapter 3 introduces the models and methods from social anthropology and ancient economics that are helpful for us better to understand socioeconomic interaction in Palestine as presupposed by Luke. Here and in chapters 4 and 5 three areas are of special importance: (1) the system of exchange of goods (reciprocal, market, redistribution), (2) the system of control of this exchange (patron–client), (3) the attitudes of the peasants towards this system (the moral economy of the peasant). Chapters 4–6 apply these models to Luke's description of social structure and social and economic interaction of the village society of Jesus' Palestine.

Finally, in chapters 7–9 I draw on the models presented to study in depth three passages about the Pharisees (Luke 11:37–44; 14:7–14; 16:13–18) that bear on the issues of greed, faith, and sharing. The concluding chapter situates the emerging picture within Luke's theology, including Acts, and raises questions about the bearing of my research on contemporary issues.

Acknowledgments

This study has been greatly inspired by the seminar on "Social Sciences and the New Testament" in the Catholic Biblical Association of America. Several members of the seminar have contributed greatly to the development of my thought, above all Bruce J. Malina, Jerome H. Neyrey, S.J., John H. Elliott, and William R. Herzog II. Among other colleagues, I am especially grateful to Wayne A. Meeks at Yale University, Jacob Jervell and Bjørn Quiller at the University of Oslo, and Daniel J. Harrington, S.J., at Weston School of Theology, for helpful and suggestive criticism.

Weston School of Theology in Cambridge, Mass., generously offered me the use of its resources in two periods as visiting scholar and included me in a congenial fellowship. The manuscript was finished during a brief period as visiting scholar at the American Baptist Seminary of the West, Berkeley, California.

The Faculty of Theology at the University of Oslo has granted me two periods of leave of absence. The Norwegian Research Council for the Humanities has given me several travel grants. My colleagues at the New Testament Seminar as well as my students at the University of Oslo have been stimulating discussion partners. Finally, I want to express my gratitude to my editor, John R. Donahue, S.J., for his thorough and perceptive criticism and wise counsel, and to John A. Hollar for his support for this project in its slow process towards completion.

From all I have learned much about sharing, which is the main theme of this book. Therefore this book is dedicated to my parents, who have shared their life with me over many years.

October 1988 HALVOR MOXNES
Oslo

Abbreviations

ATR	*Anglican Theological Review*
BARev	*Biblical Archeology Review*
CBQ	*Catholic Biblical Quarterly*
CBQMS	Catholic Biblical Quarterly—Monograph Series
CD	Cairo (Geniza text of the) Damascus (Document)
ConBNT	Coniectanea Biblica, New Testament
HNT	Handbuch zum Neuen Testament
IDB	*Interpreter's Dictionary of the Bible*
IIMO	Interuniversitair Instituut voor Missiologie en Oecumenica
JAAR	*Journal of the American Academy of Religion*
JBL	*Journal of Biblical Literature*
JES	*Journal of Ecumenical Studies*
JSNT	*Journal for the Study of the New Testament*
JRelS	*Journal of Religious Studies*
JTS	*Journal of Theological Studies*
NovT	*Novum Testamentum*
NovTSup	Novum Testamentum, Supplements
NTD	Das Neue Testament Deutsch
NTS	*New Testament Studies*
Pss. Sol.	*Psalms of Solomon*
1QpHab	*Pesher on Habakkuk* from Qumran Cave 1
RAC	*Reallexikon für Antike und Christentum*
RelSRev	*Religious Studies Review*

SBLDS	Society of Biblical Literature Dissertation Series
SBLSP	Society of Biblical Literature Seminar Papers
SEÅ	*Svensk exegetisk årsbok*
SJLA	Studies in Judaism in Late Antiquity
SNTU	Studien zum Neuen Testament und seiner Umwelt
SUNT	Studien zur Umwelt des Neuen Testaments
TDNT	*Theological Dictionary of the New Testament*
THKNT	Theologischer Handkommentar zum Neuen Testament
TRE	*Theologische Real-enzyklopädie*
WUNT	Wissenschaftliche Untersuchungen zum Neuen Testament

CHAPTER 1

A Puzzle: Were the Pharisees "Lovers of Money"?

Luke 16:14

Why did Luke say that the Pharisees were "lovers of money"? This statement in Luke 16:14 is the starting point for a study of the Pharisees in Luke's writing. It is useful to read it in its context in Luke's Gospel, after the parable of the unjust steward (16:1–9) and Jesus' exposition of that parable ending with the strong declaration of the impossibility of serving two masters:

> (13) No servant can serve two masters, for either he will hate the one and love the other, or he will be devoted to the one and despise the other. You cannot serve God and mammon. (14) The Pharisees, who were lovers of money, heard all of this, and they scoffed at him. (15) But he said to them, "You are those who justify yourselves before men, but God knows your hearts; for what is exalted among men is an abomination in the sight of God." (16) The law and the prophets were until John; since then the good news of the kingdom of God is preached, and every one enters it violently. (17) But it is easier for heaven and earth to pass away, than for one dot of the law to become void. (18) Every one who divorces his wife and marries another commits adultery, and he who marries a woman divorced from her husband commits adultery.

The statement in Luke 16:14 is part of a section (16:13–18) that has caused scholars many problems,[1] but that also contains important clues to Luke's theology.

1. One problem is the unity of the passage: it consists of several sayings that appear to be loosely strung together. Another is with the function of these sayings in their present position. Finally, even the meaning of individual verses is hard to comprehend, especially vv. 14 and 16–17. See the discussion below, pp. 146–50.

In his famous study of Lukan theology, H. Conzelmann made Luke 16:16 the key to his interpretation of Luke and to his division of salvation history in Luke's work into three distinct phases, with John the Baptist as a dividing figure.[2] Although strongly disputed, his interpretation was a tour de force in Lukan studies, and marked an era of Lukan scholarship with heavy emphasis upon chronology and eschatology. His use of Luke 16:16 is an example of how a single verse can point to a very important theme within the Gospel. In a similar way the remark about the Pharisees being lovers of money is a useful starting point to understand Luke's particular interests in his description of the Pharisees.

What did Luke mean by saying that the Pharisees were "lovers of money" *(philargyroi)*? Most scholars have taken this to be a piece of historical information about the Pharisees. Consequently, their main interest has been to gather further historical evidence to support this accusation. It is difficult, however, to fit the information of Luke 16:14 into a historical account of the Pharisees. The dilemma has been most clearly stated by T. W. Manson,[3] who suggested that one should read "Sadducees" instead of "Pharisees." Manson found the accusation of being "lovers of money" totally out of character with what is historically known about the Pharisees. He gives five reasons why this accusation with more justification should be attributed to the Sadducees: (1) The Sadducees were richer and more obvious "lovers of money" than were the Pharisees. (2) The Sadducees were more likely to scoff at Jesus' teaching about heavenly treasures. (3) In Aramaic, the form "Saddiq" in 16:14 would make a play of words together with "justify," *sdq,* in 16:15. (4) The Sadducees were wealthy and proud and considered themselves to be righteous people. (5) The parable of the rich man and Lazarus would fit a Sadducean audience.

Since there is no textual evidence for this suggestion, other scholars have not accepted Manson's thesis. In his commentary on Luke, I. H. Marshall is sympathetic to Manson's suggestion but concludes, "There is sufficient evidence of the avarice of the Pharisees to make it unnecessary to suppose that there is an error

2. *The Theology of St. Luke* (New York: Harper & Brothers, 1960).

3. *The Sayings of Jesus* (London: SCM Press, 1949), 295–96.

here."[4] Marshall lists evidence for the avarice of the Pharisees. Most of his texts are culled from the collection of Strack-Billerbeck,[5] and have been used by earlier scholars who have held a similar position. What, then, have been the arguments put forward by some of the most prominent European scholars from the turn of this century?

J. Wellhausen[6] makes his point without recourse to any supporting evidence. His first argument is of a general nature, that avarice accompanies religious separatism. His second argument is more specifically related to the social structure of Palestine. He holds that the Pharisees did not belong to the lower classes, but rather to the well-to-do middle class, especially in Jerusalem. A. Loisy likewise finds that Luke describes the Pharisees as members of the bourgeois class.[7] Moreover, Loisy thinks that their theology provided a justification for their position on riches. This last motif is also developed by E. Klostermann, who suggests that it was the Pharisees' conception of a link between piety and possessions that made them scoff at the teaching of Jesus.[8] The same point is also made by M.-J. Lagrange, who uses the Essene Damascus Document as a witness that the Pharisees were accused of luxury and avarice.[9]

Among modern scholars, K. H. Rengstorff remarks that rabbinic sources give evidence that possessions and riches asserted great attraction to those who obeyed the law.[10] He does not, however, cite any evidence for this. W. Grundmann cites some evidence for rabbinic criticism of avarice among the Pharisees without further discussion of the sources.[11] In the most recent

4. *The Gospel of Luke* (Exeter: Paternoster, 1978), 625.

5. H. Strack and P. Billerbeck, *Kommentar zum Neuen Testament aus Talmud und Midrasch,* 5 vols. (Munich: Beck, 1922–56).

6. *Das Evangelium Lucae übersetzt und erklärt* (Berlin: Reimar, 1904), 89.

7. *L'Evangile selon Luc* (Paris: Nourry, 1924), 411.

8. *Das Lukasevangelium,* HNT 5 (Tübingen: J.C.B. Mohr [Paul Siebeck], 1926), 439.

9. *Evangile selon Luc* (Paris: J. Gabalda, 1921), 439.

10. *Das Evangelium nach Lukas,* NTD 3 (Göttingen, W. Ger.: Vandenhoeck & Ruprecht, 1958), 192.

11. *Das Evangelium nach Lukas,* 5th ed., THKNT 3 (Berlin: Evangelische Verlagsanstalt, 1969), 322–23.

major commentary on Luke, J. Fitzmyer appears to accept the accusation against the Pharisees as being historically accurate, but allows the possibility that their quest of money could have honorable causes.[12]

What is the actual evidence for the position that most scholars have taken, that the avarice of the Pharisees was a historical fact? Does the rabbinic and other material that has been adduced really support this position? Marshall refers to rabbinic sources quoted in Strack-Billerbeck.[13] Marshall takes *t. Menah.* 13.22 to refer to the greed of the scribes.[14] But this is not necessarily the case. In a sequence of questions, "greed" is given as the reason in answer to the questions: Why was Shilo destroyed? Why was the first temple destroyed? Why was the second temple destroyed? It is not directly identified, however, as the greed of the scribes or of the Pharisees. *B. Mes.* 73b in the Babylonian Talmud cites two rabbis from the third and fourth centuries C.E.[15] *Ter.* 8.46b in the Palestinian Talmud cites a rabbi from the third century C.E. These texts, however, cannot be used as historical proofs for the situation in the first century.

In addition to these passages, Grundmann mentions *Testament of Moses (As. Mos.)* 7.3–8, a passage that contains accusations against a group of people for greed, self-righteousness, gluttony, and so forth.[16] The most common scholarly opinion now is that this document originated in the first century C.E., probably within the Hasidic movement; some scholars hold that it is of Pharisaic origin.[17] Thus, it is most unlikely that the text should be a criticism of these faults among Pharisees. One should rather look for enemies among the Sadducees. But the very attempt to identify historical

12. "Whether one explains the Pharisaic quest of money as a sign of God's reward for upright conduct and piety [E. Klostermann, *Lukasevangelium,* 166] or as a means enabling one to give alms to the poor [J. M. Creed, *The Gospel according to St. Luke* (London: Macmillan & Co., 1930), 206] matters little." *The Gospel according to Luke (X–XXIV),* Anchor Bible (New York: Doubleday & Co., 1985), 1112.

13. *Gospel of Luke,* 625.

14. *Gospel of Luke,* 625; quoted in Str.-B. I, 937.

15. Quoted in Str.-B. II, 222.

16. *Lukas,* 322–23.

17. J. Priest, Introduction to "Testament of Moses," from *The Old Testament Pseudepigrapha,* vol. 1, ed. J. H. Charlesworth (New York: Doubleday & Co., 1983), 920–22.

groups from these accusations is misguided. A quotation from this text bears this out:

> When this has taken place, the time will quickly come to an end. . . . Then will rule destructive and godless men, who represent themselves as being righteous, but who will [in fact] arouse their inner wrath, for they will be deceitful men, pleasing only themselves, false in every way imaginable, [such as] loving feasts at every hour of the day—devouring, gluttonous. [text is broken] But really they consume the goods of the [poor], saying their acts are according to justice. (*As. Mos.* 7.1–6)

The enemies are identifed as wealthy and connected with the temple, and similar attacks against an avaricious priesthood are found in the Qumran material as well.[18] In his commentary on this passage, however, J. Priest strikes a cautionary note: "One should be cautious in attempting to identify precisely as documents of this type tend to use stereotyped language for both praise and vilification."[19] Consequently, in no instance can it be proved that the accusations of greed are directed against the Pharisees as a historical group. Moreover, one must realize that the accusations in these texts are not historical "facts"; rather, they are polemics and elaborations of traditional motifs.

It appears, therefore, that the scholars cited above have continued an uncritical treatment of a New Testament passage strongly negative of the Pharisees, in a way they would not treat other questions in the New Testament. They have phrased the issue in historical terms, asking, Were the Pharisees really lovers of money? rather than asking the literary question, What did Luke intend by this statement? Thus, they have perpetuated unfounded criticism against the Pharisees. Furthermore, they have based their criticism on the false assumption that the rabbinic and other Jewish sources which they quote contain historical information about the Pharisees. After Jacob Neusner's groundbreaking work on the rabbinic traditions about the Pharisees,[20] a historical-critical method similar to that used in biblical studies also must be applied

18. See CD 2:12–20; 6:12–17; 20:20–27; 1QpHab 8:8–13; 11:4–15; 12:1–10; as well as *Pss. Sol.* 1; 2; 4; 8.

19. "Testament of Moses," 930; see n. 17 above.

20. *The Rabbinic Tradition about the Pharisees before 70 A.D.*, 3 vols. (Leiden, Neth.: E. J. Brill, 1971).

to rabbinic material. When dealing with this material, one must first ask, Whose interest is served by a story, a law, or a saying? What is the bias, the polemical intent of an author?[21]

Consequently, it is clear that we must start by asking not the historical question, but rather, Is Luke here using traditional language, a *topos?* And if so, what is the role of this *topos* within the larger structure of Luke's narrative?

It appears that in addition to Jewish material Luke also had Greek material as part of the background for his accusation. "Greed" *(philargyria)* occurred frequently in Hellenistic lists of vices; there was also a much-used maxim, quoted in 1 Tim. 6:6: "For the love of money *(philargyria)* is the root of all evil." The combination of this vice with that of love of honor is attested as early as the works of Plato. In Plato's discussion of who should rule the state,[22] he regards those who are covetous of honor *(philotimoi)* or covetous of money *(philargyroi)* to be unfit. Therefore, the good man must be pressed into service under pressure of penalty.

There is, however, a yet more specific use of this theme that fits well with Luke's use. The accusation against the Pharisees—that they were greedy *(philargyroi)* and that they justified themselves *(dikaiountes)* before men—echoes a popular theme in Hellenistic polemics against "false teachers." In the *Discourses* of Dio Chrysostom, written a little later than the Gospel of Luke, it is a recurrent theme in polemics against Cynics and Sophists. Dio contrasts the Cynics and the true philosophers, saying that the Cynics teach "with a view to their own profit and reputation, and not to improve you" (32.10). In another discourse, he contrasts the Sophists, who "won marvellous acclaim" and "amassed much wealth," and Socrates, who, although he was poor, "was not driven by his poverty to accept anything" (54.1–3). After their deaths, however, there was a reversal of fortunes: the Sophists had received reputation and wealth in this life, but their words perished, whereas Socrates was poor and without fame, but his words endured. Dio gives this picture of the true philosopher, as a man who

21. Jacob Neusner, *From Politics to Piety: The Emergence of Pharisaic Judaism* (Englewood Cliffs, N.J.: Prentice-Hall, 1973), 7.

22. *Republic* I.347.

"in plain terms and without guile speaks his mind with frankness, and neither for the sake of reputation *(doxēs charin)* nor for gain *(ep argyriō)* makes false pretensions, but out of good will and concern for his fellowmen stands ready, if need be, to submit to ridicule and to the disorder and uproar of the mob" (32.11). In one discourse Dio introduces himself to his audience in this way: "I have come before you not to display my talents as a speaker, nor because I want money *(argyriou)* from you; or expect your praise *(epainon)*" (35.1).

Similarly, Philo says of a "false teacher" that he "boasts of his own teaching power, . . . and in fact is filled with vanity, and demands huge fees from those who wish to attend his courses" (*Praem.* 127). In an exposition of Genesis 9 he also connects love of money with love of glory and honor (*Gig.* 37).

That the true teacher does not covet money or honor is a theme that was early taken up by Christians.[23] Paul uses it of himself when he says, "For we never used either words of flattery, as you know, or a cloak for greed *(pleonexias),* as God is witness; nor did we seek glory *(doxan)* from men . . . " (1 Thess. 2:5–6). Paul's self-sufficiency and independence of support, because he worked "with his own hands," is an important aspect of his image as a missionary.[24] When Luke takes up the theme of Paul's independence of wealth and fame, it is also in contrast to "false prophets." Paul warns the elders of the church in Ephesus against "fierce wolves" who will come, and then goes on to describe himself in his farewell speech: "I coveted no one's silver *(argyriou)* or gold or apparel. You yourselves know that these hands ministered to my necessities, and to those who were with me" (Acts 20:33–34). The vice of moneyloving is a recurrent theme in polemics against false teachers in the pastoral letters as well (1 Tim. 6:5; 2 Tim. 3:2; Tit. 1:11).[25] Luke T. Johnson has argued that "polemical language is frequently employed, not to establish the credentials of the writer

23. G. Delling, *"pleonexia," TDNT* 6:272–73.

24. See R. Hock, *The Social Context of Paul's Ministry* (Philadelphia: Fortress Press, 1980), 50–65.

25. R. J. Karris, "The Background and Significance of the Polemic of the Pastoral Epistles," *JBL* 92 (1973): 549–64.

for his audience, but to provide an antithesis to the description of the ideal teacher, that is, in paraenetic or protreptic discourses."[26]

From this one can draw two conclusions: (1) The accusation against the Pharisees that they were "moneylovers" was part of a *topos* of accusations against opponents known both in Jewish and Greek polemics. In Hellenistic and early Christian discourse it was especially used of false teachers. (2) This accusation was frequently combined with that of seeking glory, honor, and praise from men, that is, the same accusation that Jesus makes in Luke 16:15, that the Pharisees want to look righteous before men.

Thus, this material suggests that the accusations in 16:14–15 should not be discussed in terms of whether they were historically accurate, but as a literary motif in Luke. But did Luke use a well-known Hellenistic *topos* in this particular instance only, or was it part of a pattern within the literary structure of Luke's narrative? That is, does Luke's accusation of the Pharisees as moneylovers fit his general picture of them? Is it, so to speak, "in character"? It is well known that the phrase in 16:15, "You are those who justify yourselves *(dikaiountes)* before men," is part of Luke's redaction. It is a theme that he introduces in several instances to characterize the opponents of Jesus, especially scribes and Pharisees (10:29; 18:9, 14; 20:20). It is not unreasonable to think that the same is true of the theme of "moneyloving" in 16:14 as well. In fact, this has been successfully argued by Johnson.[27]

It is worth noting, however, that this approach is not without its precursors among earlier scholars. Th. Zahn,[28] writing around 1900, makes an observation of a literary character. He comments that as a general rule, the Pharisees whom Jesus met were avaricious. This is reflected in the speeches Jesus directed against them and in the parables: the home of the Pharisee in Luke 14 was a rich home; the shepherd in 15:4–6 was a well-to-do man; the forgiving father in 15:11–32 was a large landowner; and the men in 16:1 and 19 are explicitly described as rich people.

26. "1–2 Timothy and the Polemic against False Teachers: A Reexamination," *JRelS* 6/2 and 7/1 (1978–79): 4.

27. *The Literary Function of Possessions in Luke-Acts*, SBLDS 39 (Missoula, Mont.: Scholars Press, 1977).

28. *Das Evangelium Lucas*, 4th ed. (Leipzig, 1920), 570.

Thus, the next task will be to study the overall picture of the Pharisees in Luke, to see if the picture of the "moneylovers" in 16:14 fits into the larger narrative scheme of Luke's presentation of the Pharisees.

CHAPTER 2

Pillars of Society? The Role of the Pharisees in Luke's Gospel

What is the function of the Pharisees in the Gospel narrative of Luke? Where do the Pharisees fit in his description of Palestinian society in terms of social, economic, political, and religious power and control?

These questions differ from three more commonly discussed questions concerning the Pharisees in Luke. The first one is the historical question: What value does Luke have as a historical source for the question of the position and identity of the Pharisees in the first Christian century? The second frequently discussed topic is related to the synoptic question: What are the similarities and dissimilarities between the descriptions of the Pharisees in Mark, Matthew, and Luke? Third, and finally, related to these questions is that of Luke's use of the descriptions of the Pharisees: Are they a disguise for his criticism of groups within the church of his own time?

All of these are relevant and valid questions. But they cannot be answered before the literary question has been sufficiently resolved: How does Luke in his narrative describe the Pharisees within the setting of Palestinian society? A brief look at these other questions, however, is in order before we concentrate on the description of the Pharisees in Luke's Gospel.

THE HISTORICAL QUESTION: WHO WERE THE PHARISEES?

The role of the Pharisees in Judaism in the first century C.E. has been much discussed. One reason is that the historical question of the nature of Pharisaic Judaism in the first century has been linked to the discussion of the nature of present-day Judaism in comparison with Christianity. This has contributed to partly apologetic and polemical overtones in the discussion of historical issues.[1] Overcoming these flaws, the most influential studies of the history and tradition of the Pharisees in recent years have been the works of Jacob Neusner. In one major work, *The Rabbinic Traditions about the Pharisees before 70 A.D.*,[2] and in many other important studies, Neusner has argued that the Pharisees in the first century C.E. were primarily a sect concerned with purity rules, above all rules related to food and meals. This picture is a result of his historical-critical studies of the sources for the tradition of the Pharisees: rabbinic writings, Josephus, and the Gospels. The rabbinic writings and the Synoptic Gospels, according to Neusner, agree in many aspects of their picture of the Pharisees as mainly concerned with purity laws. Josephus describes the Pharisees as a political party, particularly in their initial period, while the tradition was continued by individual Pharisees in the first century.

All sources portray the Pharisees in a way which reflects their own interests, so that their pictures of the Pharisees actually reveal more about themselves than about the "historical" Pharisees.

The most probable picture of the development of the Pharisees as a group is that they wielded considerable political influence under the Maccabees. With the decline of the power of the Maccabees, however, the political influence of the Pharisees also diminished. In the first century C.E. they were first and foremost a faction within Israel bent upon observing ritual purity and trying to make the rest of Israel do the same. Then, following the destruction of the temple in 70 C.E. and the reorganization of Jewish institutions, they again came into prominence and wielded influence and power, partly due to cooperation with the Romans and partly as they became the leaders of "normative Judaism."

THE PHARISEES IN RECENT DISCUSSION

The most commonly held view is that Mark's picture of the Pharisees has been reworked by the two other Synoptic authors: by

1. See the reviews by M. J. Cook ("Jesus and the Pharisees—The Problem As It Stands Today," *JES* 15 [1978]: 441–60) and P. Culbertson ("Changing Christian Images of the Pharisees," *ATR* 64 [1982]: 539–61).

2. 3 vols. (Leiden, Neth.: E. J. Brill, 1971).

Matthew to strengthen criticism against the Pharisees, by Luke to reduce it. This has recently been argued by J. A. Ziesler[3] and J. T. Sanders.[4] Ziesler focuses primarily upon changes that Luke makes in material from tradition, and upon the tendency of material that is peculiar to Luke, most significantly several meal scenes. In his initial questions to the interpretation of meal scenes, Ziesler is commendably prudent when he questions the meaning of this typically Lukan setting: "Either Luke is modifying his anti-Pharisaic material by inserting it into such contexts, or he is doing the reverse, i.e., modifying a tradition which makes Jesus a regular guest of Pharisees by saying in effect, Yes, but see how he puts them in their place."[5] But when it comes to his conclusions, these alternatives are forgotten, and Ziesler always takes the passage as a proof of Luke's more positive view of the Pharisees. Sometimes his questions are purely historical and totally neglect a literary aspect of the function of the Pharisees within Luke's larger narrative. His method is source criticism and narrow comparison of details in the Synoptic Gospels, and thus, unsatisfactory for the purpose of interpreting the role of the Pharisees within Luke's Gospel as a whole.

Sanders's study is more ambitious in that he wants to study Luke's picture of the Pharisees both in the Gospel and in Acts. He finds that Luke has reduced the number of controversies that were found in the Gospels of Matthew and Mark. When he has introduced new material, its focus is upon controversies over *halakah:* purity of meals in terms of cleansing vessels and hands, and "clean" company, that is, nonsinners. Sanders, too, glides back and forth between literary questions and historical ones; moreover, he tries to identify the Pharisees whom Luke describes as the legalistic Pharisees of his own time, who try to impose observance of the law upon non-Jewish Christians. Sanders finds that the Pharisees in the Gospel "are the prototypes of the Christian Phar-

3. "Luke and the Pharisees," *NTS* 25 (1978): 146–57.

4. "The Pharisees in Luke-Acts," in *The Living Text: Essays in Honor of E. W. Saunders*, ed. D. E. Groh and R. Jewett (Lanham, Md.: University Press of America, 1985), 141–88. See now also J. T. Sanders, *The Jews in Luke-Acts* (Philadelphia: Fortress Press, 1987).

5. "Luke," 150.

isees in Acts 15:5 who likewise advise that those desiring admission to the church should strictly follow the Law of Moses and not rely merely on their 'belief' (Luke 7:50) to get in,"[6] and he concludes,

> Everything in Luke's portrait of the Pharisees in the Gospel conforms to this pattern, and nothing contradicts it. Only in Acts does a different picture emerge, where there are non-Christian Pharisees who help the church when they can. These Pharisees, however—along with Paul's Pharisaism—help Luke to show the bridge, the link, the continuity between the religion of the "Old Testament" and Christianity.[7]

Sanders has succeeded in linking the description of the Christian Pharisees of Acts 15:5 to the legalistic, self-righteous Pharisees of the Gospel. His interpretation is focused exclusively upon the Pharisees' relations to the law, however, and governed by his interest to identify the Pharisees with opponents in Luke's own days. Elements that cannot be subsumed under this perspective are of little interest to Sanders, so that material pertaining to the socioeconomic position of the Pharisees goes unheeded. Consequently, he has focused exclusively upon Luke's interest in the law, to the exclusion of Luke's equally strong emphasis on socioeconomic justice, and therefore misses the integration of the two elements that is so vital to Luke.

When Sanders does notice the description of the Pharisees as "lovers of money" as a Lukan redactional comment, he does not know how to make sense out of it, and gives up any attempt to interpret it.

> Finally, the Pharisaic "deriding" of Jesus in Luke 16:14 lacks a meaningful context and appears groundless. Jesus' preceding saying (v. 13) about human inability to serve two masters could hardly have been objectionable to either real or Lucan Pharisees. Furthermore, Luke's slander that they are *philargyroi* is without basis in the Gospel or the Acts. We learn from this brief statement, therefore, that Luke has a profound dislike for Pharisees and that he thinks of them as making light of Jesus, but the grounds for both escape us.[8]

Thus, Sanders's picture of the Pharisees in Luke remains in-

6. "Pharisees," 181.
7. Ibid., 184.
8. Ibid., 155–56.

complete. It is the purpose of this study to find the "meaningful context" of Luke's criticism of the Pharisees as "lovers of money," to show that it was not an isolated and groundless saying within the larger perspective of the Lukan narrative.

Neusner has summarized well the secured results of historical and synoptic studies of the Pharisees in the Gospels: "The stress of the Gospels seems just about right: cleanness laws, agricultural taboos, Sabbath and festival observances, family law."[9] The individual Gospels, however, provide a specific context for these common features, and it is this combination of motives that must be set within the complete narrative and the plot of each Gospel.

The Pharisees cannot be seen in isolation, however. They form but one group among the various groups of opponents to Jesus. Thus, we must ask, How does the author distinguish between the Pharisees and other groups of opponents? How important is their role within the opposition to Jesus as a whole? Furthermore, if the opponents are the "negative figures," how much is their picture influenced by the portrait of the "positive figures" of each Gospel, that is, Jesus and his followers?

THE PHARISEES IN MARK'S GOSPEL

Several characteristics in the description of the Pharisees in Mark's Gospel reappear in the other Synoptic Gospels. Most notable is the marked difference between the composition of the groups of opponents in the first ten chapters compared to that of the passion narrative. In the passion narrative as well as in the predictions of the Passion, Jesus' main opponents are the chief priests *(archiereis)*, the scribes *(grammateis)*, and the elders *(presbyteroi)*.[10] The elders and the chief priests, however, do not play any role in the pre-passion narrative. In these earlier parts of Mark's Gospel the adversaries of Jesus are the scribes, the Pharisees, and in a few instances, the Herodians and the Sadducees.[11]

9. "Two Pictures of the Pharisees: Philosophical Circle or Eating Club," *ATR* 64 (1982): 530.

10. Mark 8:31; 11:27; 14:43, 53; 15:1; "chief priests and scribes" only: 10:33; 11:18; 14:1; 15:31.

11. For the following, see M. J. Cook, *Mark's Treatment of the Jewish Leaders*, NovTSup 51 (Leiden, Neth.: E. J. Brill, 1978). Cook postulates that Mark had three different sources with different groups of leaders. The first one is the passion

The scribes are the most important group in Mark's Gospel. There are actually two types of scribes—on the one hand, the "Pharisaic scribes";[12] on the other hand, those associated with the chief priests and the elders—but the latter group does not have a distinctive profile of its own. In his study of the Jewish leadership in Mark's Gospel, M. J. Cook suggests that the scribes are a literary construction by Mark. They were prominent in his sources and he used them to construct "typical figures" of the Jewish leaders in his Gospel. Cook's reconstruction of Mark's sources is open for discussion;[13] the most important aspect of his interpretation, however, is the way he sees the picture of the scribes as a literary construction and a result of Mark's redaction.

In Mark's Gospel the scribes appear as the "typical" group of opponents to Jesus. They are a part of Mark's theological and literary pattern, and cast in the role of anti-types to Jesus and his disciples.[14]

THE PHARISEES IN MATTHEW'S GOSPEL

In Matthew's Gospel, too, the opponents of Jesus are described as anti-types to Jesus and his disciples.[15] There are, however, several important changes in the composition of these groups of leaders from that in Mark's Gospel. In the passion narrative in Matthew the combination of chief priests, scribes, and elders plays a much less prominent role. Instead, Matthew has another combination, that of chief priests and elders, sometimes called the elders of the people *(presbyteroi tou laou)*.[16] This terminology is

narrative, with chief priests, scribes, and elders as one undifferentiated group. Cook labels the second source the "scribe source," with the scribes as an active group of a Pharisaic type. The third source is a Pharisean/Herodian source, and locates these opponents primarily in Galilee.

12. For instance 2:6, 16; 3:22; 7:1, 5. Mark has interpolated scribes in two instances where his sources mentioned only Pharisees (2:16; 7:1).

13. See the review by J. R. Donahue, *JBL* 99 (1980): 617–19.

14. A similar picture emerges from a brief study on Mark 12:37–40 by H. Fleddermann, "A Warning about the Scribes (Mark 12:37b–40)," *CBQ* 44 (1982): 62–67.

15. For the following, see S. van Tilborg, *The Jewish Leaders in Matthew* (Leiden, Neth.: E. J. Brill, 1972), and David E. Garland, *The Intention of Matthew 23*, NovTSup 52 (Leiden, Neth.: E. J. Brill, 1979).

16. "Chief priests and elders," 27:3, 12, 20; 28:11, 12; "chief priests and elders of the people," 21:23; 26:3, 47; 27:1.

significant and points to an important motif in Matthew: it is the people of Israel as a whole that is guilty of rejecting Jesus. In their plotting to kill Jesus the elders represent the people in its totality.[17]

As a result of this, Matthew is not concerned with a historically correct description of the different groups of opponents to Jesus. Rather, to Matthew they are all basically the same. They typify and embody the opposition to Jesus and the final rejection of him.[18] Matthew, however, does not emphasize the specific characteristics of the Pharisees over against other groups. Rather, he combines the Pharisees and the Sadducees,[19] two groups that in Mark's and Luke's Gospels appear as antagonists. The main characteristic of both groups is their teaching.[20] Matthew's emphasis is not upon the characteristics of each group of leaders in Israel but upon their unanimous rejection of Jesus. In his criticism, Matthew focuses upon their role as teachers. Matthew 23 portrays the Pharisees and the scribes as teachers, sitting on the chair of Moses (23:2). But they are false teachers. When Matthew says that they sit on the chair of Moses it is not so much a recognition of their authority as a heightening of his polemics.

This emphasis upon the role of the opponents of Jesus as teachers (see also 15:1–20) corresponds to Matthew's picture of Jesus as the true teacher of Israel,[21] and puts them in the role of anti-types to Jesus. Moreover, they are also anti-types to the disciples of Jesus, who also are sent out to teach (28:16–20).

Matthew does not portray the opponents of Jesus with historical accuracy, but rather casts them in the role of "anti-types," modeled after the main characteristics of Jesus and his disciples. David E. Garland has convincingly argued that the function of this construct of the Pharisees is a warning to Christian leaders in Matthew's community.[22]

17. See esp. 22:43 and 27:25.

18. Compared to Mark there are fewer instances in which the scribes are the opponents, and the Pharisees are mentioned more frequently. Matthew replaces Mark's "scribes" with "Pharisees" in five instances. In four instances "scribes" disappear altogether. In four other instances, however, Matthew introduces "scribes" where Mark did not have them. Finally, "Pharisees" are introduced in four instances.

19. 3:7; 16:1, 6, 11, 12.

20. 16:5, 11, 12.

21. Cf. 5—7; 23:8–10.

22. *The Intention of Matthew 23*, 117–23.

THE PHARISEES IN LUKE'S GOSPEL

If Luke shows the same pattern as Mark and Matthew, we shall expect him to cast the opponents in the role of anti-types to Jesus and his disciples. Consequently, we also need to raise the question of the main characteristics of Luke's description of Jesus and his disciples. It is with this picture of Jesus and his disciples that the portrayal of Jesus' opponents needs to be contrasted. It is more important to grasp how the opponents of Jesus function within Luke's narrative and theology than to make a minute comparison with parallel statements by Mark and Matthew.[23] The Pharisees, too, must be studied within the total picture of the opponents to Jesus in Luke's work. Do they blend into a homogeneous group of opponents, or does Luke ascribe a specific and distinctive function to them?

The composition of the groups of opponents in Luke's work is different from that in Mark's and Matthew's. The strict pattern in Mark's Gospel, with one group of opponents in the pre-passion narrative and another group in the passion narrative, is broken. In Luke the fixed groups become fragmented, and there are a number of new groups or individuals among the opponents. For instance, in the passion narrative we hear of officers (*stratēgoi,* 22:4, 52) and rulers (*archòntes,* 23:13; 24:20). The chief priests, however, still occupy a significant role in this section, but frequently in cooperation with other groups.[24] In the pre-passion narrative as well, there are a number of new groups, lawyers (*nomikoi,* 10:25; 11:45, 46, 52) and teachers of law (*nomodidaskaloi,* 5:17), in addition to the familiar groups from Mark and Matthew: Pharisees, scribes, and Sadducees.

In many instances, it is not possible to distinguish between the various groups in terms of function and characteristics. For instance, in 11:37–54 Pharisees, lawyers, and scribes appear, if not as identical groups, at least very much alike in that they face the same accusations. Likewise, the accusations leveled against the Phar-

23. See J. B. Tyson, "The Opposition to Jesus in the Gospel of Luke," *Perspectives in Religious Studies* 5 (1978): 144–50.

24. E. J. Via, "According to Luke, Who Put Jesus to Death?" in *Political Issues in Luke-Acts*, ed. R. J. Cassidy and P. J. Scharper (Maryknoll, N.Y.: Orbis Books, 1983), 129–33.

isees in 11:43 run parallel to those addressed to the scribes in 20:45–47. One point, however, about which Luke is quite emphatic, is that the Pharisees are clearly distinguishable from the Sadducees because of their belief in the resurrection of the dead (20:27–40; Acts 23:6–10).

There is a significant increase, however, in passages referring to the Pharisees, compared to Mark and Matthew. This holds true of the Pharisees both mentioned alone (7:36; 13:31; 14:1; 16:14; 17:20; 18:10–14) and combined with other groups such as scribes (11:53) or lawyers and teachers of law (5:17; 7:30; 14:3). All these occurrences are outside of the passion narrative, in which the Pharisees are not mentioned. In Luke's pre-passion narrative, however, the Pharisees clearly are the most important faction among the opponents of Jesus. J. B. Tyson reaches a similar conclusion: "It appears that Luke thinks in terms of two complexes of opposing groups: one gathered around Pharisees, and the other around chief priests, with scribes interacting with both."[25]

The Pharisees dominate the scene outside of Jerusalem, starting with Galilee. Mark and Matthew describe the Pharisees who came to Jesus at the Gennesaret Sea as coming from Jerusalem (Matt. 15:1; Mark 7:1). To Luke, however, the Pharisees are natives of Galilee; he describes them as coming to hear Jesus "from every village of Galilee and Judea and from Jerusalem" (5:17). This is part of Luke's emphasis that people came from all over the country to hear Jesus.

Luke is not clear in his descriptions of the geography of Palestine. One has the feeling that he sees the country from afar, with little interest in detail and writing for readers without detailed knowledge of the area. This is particularly true of the travel narrative (9:51—19:27). Jerusalem as the goal for the journey provides the geographical and theological center of the narrative, and also determines its literary structure.[26] The details of Jesus' long journey from Galilee via Samaria (9:51–56) and Judea to Jerusalem are obscure.[27] Luke's interest obviously lies elsewhere: in the

25. "Opposition," 149.

26. See 9:51; 13:33–35; 17:11; 18:31; 19:11, 28, 41–45.

27. After a long journey starting in 9:51, Luke 17:11 describes Jesus as still passing along "between Samaria and Galilee."

double motif of Jesus being "on his way" and of discipleship as a following of Jesus. His interest in geography is partly political: he is aware of administrative areas (2:1–2; 3:1–2), and his interest in Galilee seems to be connected with the role of Herod in the Passion of Jesus (3:1; 13:31–35; 23:6–12).

Although Luke is not clear on divisions between the various regions of Palestine,[28] it is quite clear that he situates the Pharisees in all parts of the country, spread through towns and villages. Although he mentions that they came also from Jerusalem (5:17), they never actually play any role in the passion narrative. That some Pharisees were in the crowds at Jesus' entry into Jerusalem is a recurrent theme from the Galilean scene and the travel narrative. In the crowds that followed Jesus, then, there were also Pharisees. Moreover, Luke emphasizes that the Pharisees lived permanently in Galilee and Judea outside of Jerusalem by focusing his interest on their use of their homes for hospitality.

In a feature characteristic of Luke, he portrays Pharisees as hosts to Jesus in their houses (7:36–50; 11:37; 14:1–14). At least some of the Pharisees are rich. With Luke's use of "typical figures," we can assume that the description of the Pharisee who was a rich ruler (*archōn,* 14:1) functions as a *topos*. Parables or stories addressed to the Pharisees yield a similar picture: the parables of the great banquet (14:15–24), of the dishonest steward (16:1–9), of the rich man and Lazarus (16:19–31), and of the Pharisee and tax collector in the temple (18:10–14). Thus, Luke's interest in the meal scenes is not merely in a discussion of purity laws as such;[29] the issue of ritual purity is put within a much broader context of justice and the coming of the kingdom. In his discussion of religious teachings and practices that affected everyday life, Luke's focus is on ritual purity, faith in God, and social interaction on a local level (11:37–43; 14:7–14; 16:14–18).

This interest in the Pharisees in the villages affecting people's daily life raises the question of how Luke perceives the relations between the Pharisees and the ordinary villagers, the people. In

28. Some of the confusion is caused by his using "Judea" sometimes for the province, and sometimes for the whole Jewish area (23:5; Acts 10:37; probably also in Luke 4:31; 6:17; 7:17).

29. As J. T. Sanders in "The Pharisees in Luke-Acts" appears to think.

some ways Luke seems to pit them against each other. This conflict becomes visible in their attitude towards John the Baptist (7:29–30) and Jesus. The dual response to Jesus' eulogy of John in 7:29–30 has programmatic character:

> When they heard all this all the people and the tax collectors justified God, having been baptized with the baptism of John; but the Pharisees and the lawyers rejected the purpose of God for themselves, not having been baptized by him.

Here we find the common people and the outcasts on the one side, the Pharisees on the other. This statement also provides a link to John's preaching of conversion, with Luke's special emphasis on justice (3:10–14), as well as a link to the combined sayings about the Pharisees and about John in 16:14–16.

The context of Luke 7:29–30 also provides a clue to a major motif in Luke's description of Jesus, as it is brought out in Jesus' answer to John the Baptist's question: "Are you he who is to come?" (7:19):

> Go and tell John what you have seen and heard: the blind receive their sight, the lame walk, lepers are cleansed, and the deaf hear, the dead are raised up, the poor have good news preached to them. And blessed is he who takes no offense at me. (7:22–23)

This answer has its parallel in Matt. 11:4–6. In the Lukan context, however, it takes on a new significance due to its link to Jesus' programmatic speech in Nazareth, focusing on the good news for the poor, the prisoners, and the sick (4:16–19), as well as its link to Jesus' reversal speech in 6:20–26. Thus, these texts focus on Jesus as the fulfiller of God's promise of justice and salvation for the downtrodden. This lends credence to the argument by F. W. Danker that the basic model for Luke's picture of Jesus is that of a benefactor.[30] Based on the Hellenistic image of the king as the benefactor of his people, Luke's Jesus appears as the benefactor of the world, carrying out God's work of salvation and sustenance. In a similar way the disciples continue the works of Jesus to heal and to minister.

30. *Luke,* Proclamation Commentary (Philadelphia: Fortress, 1976), 6–17. See also F. W. Danker, *Benefactor: Epigraphic Study of a Graeco-Roman and New Testament Semantic Field* (St. Louis: Clayton, 1982).

As we have seen with Matthew and Mark, this Lukan role of Jesus and of his disciples is reflected in the description of the opponents in a negative way. Compared to the emphasis on teaching as the main characteristic of Jesus' opponents in Matthew's Gospel, Luke's picture of the Pharisees is markedly different. Luke does have parallel material to much of Matthew 23, although scattered in various chapters of his Gospel (11:37–54; 20:45–47) and with much less emphasis on the controversy over the correct teaching of the law. The Pharisees are shown in a much broader perspective with a larger social role to play: they are the main opponents of Jesus in the villages outside of Jerusalem; they are aggressive upholders of the laws of purity. Furthermore, they play an important role in the social and economic life of the village communities.

What is the function of this description of the Pharisees within Luke's narrative? A partial answer is given by Luke T. Johnson in *The Literary Function of Possessions in Luke-Acts*.[31] He found that the picture of the Pharisees as rich and "lovers of money" was part of a literary pattern of acceptance and rejection of Jesus. The poor accepted Jesus whereas the rich rejected him. Consequently, since the Pharisees rejected Jesus, it was part of the picture that they were also rich and that they loved money instead of God.

While useful, this literary study only gives a partial answer to the function of the Pharisees in Luke's work. First of all, we must raise the question of the social context that gave meaning to this picture of the Pharisees as "moneylovers." How does Luke describe Palestinian society and its social and economic interaction? How does he see the Pharisees and their function vis-à-vis the people who flocked to Jesus—the common villagers as well as the outcasts of the local communities? Where do the Pharisees fit in this society as it is described by Luke?

31. 109–10, 139–40.

CHAPTER 3

Ancient Economy and Social Interaction

Luke's statements about the Pharisees, that they were rich or moneylovers, as well as his other statements about money and possessions, are not isolated expressions. Rather, they are integral to his Gospel and part of a larger pattern of social, moral, and cosmological relations that make up the society that he describes.

How shall we gain access to information about Luke's social and economic system? There is more explicit information in his Gospel than in any of the other Gospels. But even this wealth of material does not by itself constitute a system or show the dynamics of the system. A listing of all information about money, occupations, spending patterns, buying, and selling does not tell us what it means. This information must be put within a framework that explains its meaning. It is not valid to use our present-day societies as a model, as we unconsciously are prone to do. Not only was Luke's society not industrialized and without a middle class, but "economy" itself was a totally different factor in his society. Thus, we need a framework, a model that is fitted for Luke's description of Palestinian society, that is, an agrarian society within the Hellenistic world in the eastern part of the Roman Empire in the first century.

NEW TESTAMENT AND SOCIAL SCIENCE METHODS

The use of social science models in the study of the New Testament has been much discussed in recent years and does not need any further justification in a general sense.[1] In a more specific sense, however, there is a question of what problem one addresses, and whether models from social sciences will be of help for that particular problem. For instance, if one studies the Old Testament roots of Luke's Christology, sociology or social anthropology is hardly relevant. In a study of the social and economic relations between the Pharisees and the village population, as Luke describes them, it is quite obvious that economics, social anthropology, sociology, as well as history and more traditional areas, are useful. Then it becomes a matter of relevant methods and models. For instance, models from social anthropology seem more relevant than models from sociology, because the former are mostly based on preindustrialized societies. Moreover, the mutual interdependence of social anthropology and fields such as ancient history, economics, and archeology proves the usefulness of anthropological models in historical studies.

The goal for this study is to offer something similar on Luke to what Moses I. Finley did on Homer's *Odyssey* in *The World of Odysseus*. His goal was to create

> a picture of society, based on a close reading of the Iliad and Odyssey, supported by study of other societies to help elucidate obscure points in the poems. The social institutions and values make up a coherent system, and from our present outlook, a very alien one, but neither an improbable nor an unfamiliar one in the experience of modern anthropology.[2]

It is a similar close reading that this study will attempt to accomplish. In this we are more concerned with the typical and recurring than with the singular and historical. For instance, Luke does not give a historically accurate description of Jesus' travels in his travel narrative (Luke 9:51—19:27). But that is of no great importance to us when we ask how Luke describes the social interaction in the villages that Jesus visits. Another question of a historical nature concerns Luke's knowledge of Palestine at the time of Jesus. How

1. For theoretical discussions, as well as application of methods on individual passages, see the collection of studies in *Semeia* 35 (1986): "Social-Scientific Criticism of the New Testament and Its Social World."

2. *The World of Odysseus*, rev. ed. (Harmondsworth, Eng.: Penguin Books, 1965), 9.

much did he know, for instance, about the geography of Palestine? To what extent was his historical narrative influenced by his attempts to relate the story to readers of his own time? These are very important questions in attempts to locate Luke culturally and geographically. When it comes to identifying patterns of social and economic relations in the narratives, however, a difference in time of maybe fifty to sixty years, or among various localities in the eastern Mediterranean, is not so crucial. These were patterns that did not change quickly in antiquity, so it is rather a matter of using models from social anthropology and ancient economics that are appropriate for the period and for the eastern Mediterranean area during the early Roman Empire. Within these basic patterns, however, we may be able to discern regional and cultural differences.

Traditional historical-critical methods such as source criticism, form criticism, and redaction criticism do not play an important part in this study. They are geared more toward the historical questions, be they of the historical Jesus or of Luke and his addressees. Therefore, they are not as helpful for the purpose of this study, which is to approach the Pharisees and their role within the social structure of Palestinian society as Luke depicts it. Thus, the primary interest is that of the narrative as Luke construed it in its totality, basing his work on written sources, Mark and Q, as well as on sources particular to him. This approach is similar to that in a growing number of Lukan studies that are more attuned to literary criticism and a holistic perspective than traditional redaction criticism.[3] The main emphasis, therefore, is upon the narrative in its totality, not just the redactional activity by Luke. At the same time Luke's redaction is important, because it points to his intentions in rendering the narrative the way he did, and we therefore would do well to look to his redactional comments for perspective in reading his story.

Luke stands within an ancient tradition of writing history with a

3. Cf. C. H. Talbert, *Reading Luke: A Literary and Theological Commentary on the Third Gospel* (New York: Crossroad, 1982), and R. C. Tannehill, *The Narrative Unity of Luke-Acts,* vol. 1, *The Gospel according to Luke* (Philadelphia: Fortress Press, 1986).

specific purpose.[4] The history that he wrote stands within the framework of his theology (1:1–4). Therefore, the narratives are in a certain way "transparent," in that they intend not only to describe Jesus and his followers, but also to address listeners and readers at Luke's own time. This makes historical reconstruction from the narratives difficult, be it attempts to reconstruct the situation of Jesus (form criticism) or that of Luke and his audience (redaction criticism). But as already stated, we are not attempting to reconstruct a particular historical situation, but rather a pattern of *typical social relations*, *economic interaction*, and *values* explicitly or implicitly presupposed in Luke's narrative.[5] Our first question concerns the role of the Pharisees, as Luke describes it.

The Pharisees: A Question of Social Relations

The attempt to describe the Lukan Pharisees in their relationship to other groups in society sets this study apart from studies of the Pharisees per se. They will not be studied as individuals or as a group independent of its surroundings. The German sociologist Norbert Elias holds it to be one of the major insights of social studies, also to be applied to historical studies, that one should study people as those who are "dependent upon others and on whom others depend—and whose interdependence can be determined by investigation."[6] The goal of this study is to go beyond an individualist approach and see the relationship between the Pharisees and the common people as a network of people who are mutually dependent, and whose relations are structured in a specific way. It is to get a picture of the specific structure of this interdependence that models are necessary.

A similar approach to the "interdependence model" of Elias is

4. See D. E. Aune, *The New Testament in Its Literary Environment* (Philadelphia: Westminster Press, 1987), 77–141.

5. This is a quest for the "social world" of Luke's Gospel. For definitions of "social world," see J. Z. Smith, "The Social Description of Early Christianity," *RelSRev* 1 (1975): 21.

6. *The Court Society* (New York: Pantheon Books, 1983), 24.

that offered by Richard L. Rohrbaugh,[7] speaking of "relational conceptions" in a discussion of methods used to determine the social class of early Christians. He takes as his starting point that in all societies there have been inequalities in the distribution of wealth, power, and privilege. It is not enough, however, just to record these inequalities. The problem is to discover the principles of their distribution and their role in social dynamics.

Rohrbaugh sets forth two main sets of theories. One is that of "graduational conceptions." This attempt to define classes is based on a division according to the "degree in which they possess the characteristics which constitute the criteria of division"[8]—for instance, income, education, or political position.

More satisfactory, however, is the theory of "relational conceptions." It is based on measuring "qualitative positions in a social relation." Thus, position is the key. People stand in a particular social relation in which the position of each individual defines the other: for instance, parent–child, creditor–debtor. One party in the relation is in control. Whereas the graduational conception was descriptive and static, the relational one is analytical, and will explain both the source of inequality and its dynamics.

It has been discussed which social relations are fundamental in producing social inequality. Class relations often have been studied in terms of their function within the market. Rohrbaugh, however, finds an analysis of class relations within the system of production useful. This analysis can be subdivided with emphasis on different areas, that of the technical division of labor, of authority relations, and of a system of exploration. Since there is not much New Testament material on the division of labor, Rohrbaugh finds an analysis in terms of "authority relations" the most useful.

A major question in antiquity was the control of surplus economic production. Control means power. Authority relations can therefore be studied in terms of power, as a relationship between dominance and subordination. An analysis of the patterns of power in society will help us understand the mechanism of social conflict and control. A broad definition of "social class" is there-

7. "Methodological Considerations in the Debate over the Social Class of Early Christians," *JAAR* 52 (1985): 519–46.

8. Ibid., 529.

fore "power group." Authority and power are not only economic; other factors such as politics, heredity, education, and so forth, are important to understanding how the control system works. In antiquity the political and the economic systems were inseparable.

Rohrbaugh suggests that the most useful approach to an analysis of "class" is to understand it broadly as "politico-economic interest group." The central concern of first-century Greco-Roman economy was to have power to control the economic system and to expropriate the surplus. A relational study of this society is analytical. How and why did the system become the way it was? It is not enough to know that somebody is rich; we also need to know how he became rich. A relational approach focuses on the relations between people in the texts. It does not merely put them on a gradational scale. The question to be asked is, What kind of relationship did a debtor have with his creditor, or day laborers with a landowner? Furthermore, this implies constantly asking the question of power. The economic system was politically controlled, and power was a means to wealth. To have wealth without power meant to be in a precarious situation. Therefore, the major locus of interest was the intersection of political power and economic system.

Elias and Rohrbaugh have put forth perspectives and theories that will be very important for our study. Yet they have not offered models that can be practiced on the texts. To that question we now turn.

ANCIENT ECONOMY EMBEDDED IN SOCIAL LIFE

Luke's description of the Pharisees as "moneylovers" suggests that we study the position of the Pharisees in Luke's narrative from the perspective of their economic role. To do this, we need to understand the role of economics within ancient societies.

All discussion of ancient economy must start from the fact that it was based on agriculture. Agriculture was not just one sector of the economy. It formed the very basis for the economy. This fact challenges not only our common economic models but our political, cultural, and social models. For instance, in an agricultural economy it is not meaningful to speak of the contrast between "urban" and "rural" in terms of "industrial" versus "agricultural." In antiquity nearly all towns were totally dependent upon the agricultural production of the land.[9] They were "preindustrial cities."[10] They were the seats of large landowners who lived on revenue from their landholdings, and of central powers like kings and priests who extracted tribute from the production of the land. This was also the way power worked. Power meant control of land and of agricultural production. Thus, it is not meaningful for this period to speak of different "sectors" of the economy. The difference between town and land is rather to be understood in terms of center versus periphery, and in terms of an unequal power relationship with much power in the center and less in the periphery. The major political question in ancient societies was, Who had the power to control the production of the land and to extract the surplus? This is the main question to keep in mind when we look at the different forms of exchange within this society and the social structure within which they were embedded.

What is an "Embedded" Economy?

No economy is totally separate from the social, political, and cultural structures of a society. That is true also in modern societies, where differences in culture may explain differences in economic development: for instance, in the United States, in Japan, and in Latin America. Social and political positions may put restraints upon the economic sector. The value put upon labor is not a result of economic factors alone; it may be part of a political decision made by a society. There is a growing awareness that the economies of our modern societies are embedded in a cultural context.[11]

Although modern economies in some ways are culturally dependent, they still very much form an independent sector of soci-

9. Moses I. Finley, *The Ancient Economy* (Berkeley and Los Angeles: University of California Press, 1973), 123–49; R. MacMullen, *Roman Social Relations* (New Haven: Yale University Press, 1974), 28–55.

10. G. Sjøberg, *The Preindustrial City* (New York: Free Press of Glencoe, 1960).

11. M. Granovetter, "Economic Action and Social Structure: The Problem of Embeddedness," *American Journal of Sociology* 91 (1985): 481–510. Notice also the recently established Institute for the Study of Economic Culture at Boston University, headed by sociologist Peter L. Berger (*Boston Globe*, July 14, 1986, 14, 16).

ety and in many instances have a controlling influence upon other sectors. For instance, in the case of multinational corporations or arms-production industry, the economy can take the form of an isolated department with its own language, rules, and power structure. Thus, there is a real difference between modern and ancient economies.

"In antiquity the political and the economic systems were inseparable."[12] This statement by Rohrbaugh points to a major difference in the role of the economy in ancient societies compared to modern, industrialized societies. In antiquity the economy was never a "sector" of society, a separate institution with its own rules. It was embedded in society and in its power structure. This structure of power ruled production and exchange systems, which therefore did not operate according to a "free market" economy. Consequently, this economy must be studied within the framework of the social organization of society as a whole.

This understanding of ancient economy is closely associated with the work of Karl Polanyi and a collection of studies, *Trade and Market in the Early Empires*.[13] These articles were seminal for later works both in the study of the economy in ancient civilizations, and of present-day peasant and tribal societies. Thus, the study of ancient economies and that of modern economic anthropology are interrelated so as to make inferences from one discipline useful within the other. In this study both disciplines have proved useful.

Polanyi sums up in a brief paragraph his explanation of what it means to say an economy is "embedded":

> The human economy, then, is embedded and enmeshed in institutions, economic and non-economic. The inclusion of the non-economic is vital. For religion or government may be as important for the structure and functioning of the economy as monetary institutions or the availability of tools and machines themselves that lighten the toil of labor.[14]

Polanyi's scholarly view corresponded with his political views of

12. Rohrbaugh, "Social Class," 525.

13. Karl Polanyi et al., *Trade and Market in the Early Empires* (1957; reprint, Chicago: Henry Regnery, 1971).

14. Ibid., 250.

the function of economy in society. S. C. Humphreys says of him that

> [his] work was based on the political conviction that the function of economy should be to strengthen social relationships and eliminate conflict by an allocation of wealth conforming to the values of each society. The subordination of economic organization to social ends . . . was for Polanyi a feature of all societies except that dominated by modern market economy.[15]

Within anthropological studies the relationship between economy and society has been elaborated by M. H. Nash.[16] He sums up the relationship in one sentence: "Economic action is only part of the system of social action." Economic action is tied in with social action in three ways: "First, by normative integration, second by functional interdependence, and third by causal interaction."

The first kind of interaction links economic activity to the value system of a society. Thus, norms governing social interaction at large also govern economic activity: "From this point of view, there are no economic motives, but only motives appropriate to the economic sphere."

Second, the functional interdependence stresses the personal aspect of the integration of the economy in the workings of society: "The same persons are actors in the economic, the kinship, the political, and the religious sphere."

Third, the provision of facilities is the main factor in the causal interaction between economy and society.

> For given forms of social structure a given variety and volume of goods and services are required, and if there are shifts in facilities available, there will be shifts in the rest of society. Conversely, shifts in the social structure will change the volume and variety of goods and services a society produces.

Here it will be useful to add some examples from the ancient world on the first point Nash makes, that there are no economic

15. "History, Economics, and Anthropology: The Work of Karl Polanyi," *Anthropology and the Greeks* (Boston and London: Routledge & Kegan Paul, 1978), 63.

16. "The Organization of Economic Life," in *Tribal and Peasant Economy*, ed. G. Dalton (1967; reprint, Austin: University of Texas Press, 1981), 3–12. The following quotes are from pp. 9, 10.

motives, only motives appropriate to the economic scene. This observation appears to fit the ancient world very well. The evidence from written sources almost exclusively informs us about the views of the elites, and it is therefore ancient economy from their perspective that is most easily accessible. T. F. Carney observes that whereas languages of antiquity had elaborate semantic fields connected with war and religion, there was none connected with economics, and therefore there was no economic theory.[17] This reflected the way in which the elites of the time thought: "The elites thought in strategic or military terms, rather than in cash-conscious or cost-benefit terms."[18]

The dominant economic unit was the extended household with an estate and household economy. Economic activity was only one of the activities of the household, and therefore subordinated to the primary goals of the household. The elites based their power on politics and status rather than on economy. The main purpose of the household economy was to allow the elite to maintain status through "conspicuous consumption." This was so at the highest levels of society, and holds true also for the Roman emperor. The economy of the elites was geared towards satisfaction of their needs, and these needs were not based on "economic considerations" in our meaning of the term.[19] More often than not these needs were political and military rather than economic. Finley disputes that wars were fought for economic reasons.[20] And Carney argues that wars were fought without considerations for the economic, social, and political problems they might cause, and that they in their turn led to endemic conflict over the distribution of goods.[21]

Compared to modern mentality there was a totally different mode of thinking that had very little incentive towards change and experimentation: "Technical progress, economic growth, productivity, even efficiency have not been significant goals since the

17. *The Shape of the Past: Models and Antiquity* (Lawrence, Kans.: Coronado, 1975), 213.

18. Ibid., 214.

19. Finley, *Ancient Economy*, 160–61.

20. Ibid., 157.

21. *Shape of the Past*, 249–50.

beginning of time."[22] Although agriculture was the main source of income, there was no incentive to increase profit through new modes of production. Instead, there was competition to increase wealth through control of more land. This was an economy based on exploitations and not on growth, and therefore, "the prevailing mentality was acquisitive not productive."[23]

This was "the moral economy" of the landowner in antiquity, and as a result there was a trend towards a steady increase in the size of landholdings throughout antiquity.[24] Later (chap. 5) we will try to trace the "moral economy of the peasant," mostly with the help of anthropological studies from present-day peasant societies, since the evidence from ancient times is so scarce. We now consider Polanyi's model for economic exchange.

A MODEL FOR ECONOMIC EXCHANGE

Polanyi was primarily interested in the exchange of goods, which he regarded as more important than the mode of production. Consequently, he used economic categories that were concerned with the allocation of goods and the organization of economic relations between social units. His categories were *reciprocity, redistribution,* and *market exchange*. Later he added *householding,* a term that does not actually fit his categories, since it does not refer to relations between units but to the economic aspect within the basic social unit.

Humphreys has provided a useful summary of Polanyi's definition of the various categories:

> Reciprocal presentations of food and other gifts, labor or hospitality occur typically between affinal groups or between neighbors. Market exchange makes transactions possible between individuals irrespective of their social relationship. Redistribution requires central collection and allocation by a higher authority, but can be seen as satisfying the basic unit's need for services and goods which it cannot produce alone by providing an institutional channel for the pooling of resources.[25]

22. Finley, *Ancient Economy*, 147.
23. Ibid., 144.
24. Ibid., 102.
25. "Polanyi," 65.

Polanyi's model of exchange has been incorporated by Nash into a more comprehensive model of the organization of economic life in peasant and primitive societies. He outlines four axes along which the prominent features of these types of economy can be measured: (1) technological complexity and the division of labor; (2) the structure and membership of productive units; (3) systems and media of exchange; and (4) the control of wealth and capital.

For the purpose of this study, systems of exchange and control of wealth are most pertinent, since it is here that social and political factors are most important. However, a comment on the structure of productive units is in order.

The Family/Kinship Group as a Productive Unit

In peasant societies production is based on social units organized not solely for the purpose of production, but for kinship, such as families, clans, and kindreds.[26] Moreover, economic activity is only one part of their various occupations. The goal of production in these units is to secure their livelihood. Both production and exchange are based on the same principle of need: "It is 'what they need': the exchange and the production for it are oriented to livelihood, not profits. . . . It is not merely 'production for use,' but production for use value, even through the acts of exchange, as opposed to the quest for exchange value."[27] This is a fundamental difference from modern economies, in which production is a "production for exchange." The difference is summed up by the anthropologist M. Sahlins in this way: "One is an economic system of determinate and finite objectives while the other holds out the infinite goal of 'as much as possible.' "[28]

The fact that the family also functions as a production unit strengthens the internal solidarity of the group. Moreover, the group is also a consumption unit that shares its resources between individual members of the group. This form of sharing within the group can be called pooling, and this is an important and necessary

26. For the following, see M. Sahlins, *Stone Age Economics* (Chicago: Aldine Publishing, 1972), 41–148.

27. Ibid., 83.

28. Ibid., 84.

function of householding. It is a constituting activity of the group; it serves to abolish differences between group members and strengthens group cohesion.

Reciprocity and Redistribution

The most important form of exchange in peasant societies is reciprocal exchange.[29] Reciprocity is a relation *between* two parties that have distinct socioeconomic interests. It aims at symmetry between the two parties. The term "reciprocity" covers a whole class of exchanges. Its particular form is heavily dependent upon the social closeness or distance between the parties involved. Sahlins presents the following schemes of reciprocities:

(1) Generalized reciprocity. This is the "solidarity extreme." This form for exchange covers transactions that are altruistic; the ideal form is the "pure gift."

(2) Balanced reciprocity. This form for exchange attempts to reach near-equivalence in goods and services. Within this form of exchange relationships between people can be disrupted if there is a failure to reciprocate for a gift received.

(3) Negative reciprocity. This is the "unsocial extreme." It designates attempts to "get something for nothing," and the ways to get it may vary from nonviolent to violent.

Modes of exchange are conditioned by the span of social distance. By close kinship, reciprocity is inclined towards general reciprocity. Where there are no kinship links—for instance, in relation to strangers—there is a tendency towards negative reciprocity. A tribe or a group can be divided in several sectors according to social distance: house, lineage sector, village sector, tribal sector, and intertribal sector. The form of reciprocity is apt to vary according to sectoral position.

Forms of reciprocity are influenced not only by kinship distance but also by kinship rank. The basic element in the rank factor is that rank is privilege and that rank in its turn carries responsibilities. Thus, from those of high rank generosity is expected. High rank—for instance, chieftainship—is often secured or sus-

29. For the following, see ibid., 185–276.

tained largely through generosity. This generosity often takes the form of generalized exchange.

Furthermore, the form of reciprocity is influenced by differences in wealth. There are certain restraints upon the wealthy as well as certain expectations, for instance, generalized exchange beyond the close kinship group.

Finally, the type of goods involved influences the form of exchange. In particular food is an important barometer of the character of exchange. Since food is necessary for the upkeep of life and so urgently needed, it is more readily given in general exchange than other goods.

Whereas reciprocity is a relation *between* two parties, redistribution is a relation *within* a group. It is based on social unity and is an expression of "centricity," movement to and from a center. The basic form of redistribution is associated with chieftainship as the simplest form of a centralized community, and it is found in all centralized groups and societies. It will be discussed in the section on centralized economy.

The Use of Money as a Medium of Exchange

In primitive and peasant economies money is neither the only nor the predominant medium of exchange. In a peasant economy, however, it plays a more important part than in a primitive economy, due to the importance of the market.[30] In both types of society traditional social organizations and cultural practices play an important role. But in a peasant economy much business concerning land and labor, as well as goods and services, is transacted through the market. Consequently, the function of money as a medium of exchange is important.

What was the effect on the culture of exchange when money was used as a medium? Aristotle attributes disastrous effects to the introduction of money into the ancient Greek economy.[31] In a system of exchange within "natural relationships," there are natu-

30. G. Dalton, "Primitive Money," in *Tribal and Peasant Economy*, 254–81.
31. *Politics* 1256*b*40–1258*a*20.

ral limits of restraints, but "when money becomes an intermediary element in exchange, the natural limits on physical wants cease to exercise restraints on desire and the unlimited desire for wealth results in a lack of natural restraints."[32] In many ways his argument is similar to the distinction between ancient and modern economy, between exchange for livelihood and exchange for profit, which was mentioned above.

The economy of the Roman Empire was on its way to becoming a money economy. But there was a difference between urban and rural economy, with the use of money probably more pervasive in towns than in the countryside.[33] Thus, the question to ask about Luke is whether he gives information about the relative importance of money as a medium of exchange, and what forms of money he mentions.

PATRON–CLIENT SOCIETIES AND THE CONTROL OF WEALTH

The fourth dimension of variation among economic systems in ancient and peasant economies is the control of wealth. In this area the link between the social system and the economy is the strongest; therefore, this question deserves a special discussion. On the village level, economic exchange mostly takes the form of reciprocity. On the level of a state or nation or an area with centralized government, economic exchange will include redistribution through some central power. But this centralized form of economic exchange also may be channeled through more reciprocal forms for exchange in patron–client relationships.

We need to distinguish between the actual power relations expressed through the control of wealth from the top in ancient societies and the "moral economy of the peasant," which attempts to put restraints on the powerful. Thus, we first focus on models for control based on the power of the elites, which was the form of power most in use in ancient societies.

32. S. Todd Lowry, "Recent Literature on Ancient Greek Economic Thought," *Journal of Economic Literature* 17 (1979): 68.

33. R. Duncan-Jones, *The Economy of the Roman Empire*, 2d ed. (Cambridge: Cambridge University Press, 1982), 7.

Exchange Controlled by an Elite

In their study *Patrons, Clients, and Friends,* S. N. Eisenstadt and L. Roniger have a chapter on "generalized exchange and the development of interpersonal relations."[34] They use the term "generalized exchange" for a means of structuring the flow of resources and social relations that differ from the "free market." They see kinship as the starting point for this form of exchange, together with other forms of ascriptive communities, for example, nations. This generalized exchange creates a certain kind of connection between the instrumental and the power relations on the one hand, and the solidarity relation and the construction of meaning on the other hand.

Thus, the generalized exchange becomes institutionalized; it is a relationship between a specific group of people. This process of institutionalization takes place in four ways: (1) there are normative specifications of what goals or desiderata are available to the members of a certain group or sociocultural category (sex, age, occupation, membership of territorial proximity); (2) it defines the basic attributes of social and cultural similarity that serve as criteria to become members, and it defines a member's privileges and duties, thus distinguishing between members and nonmembers; (3) the designation of the obligations upon members also specifies the general principles of distribution of power between them; (4) the structuring of resources and social relations implies that there is given "some higher, transcendental meaning to these collectivities and to the social activities entailed."[35]

Thus we have four questions concerning the structuring of resources through a kinship or membership group: What goals and desired goods are available to members of a certain group or sociocultural category? What are the basic social and cultural criteria to become members, and what are the members' privileges and duties? What are the general principles of distribution of power between members? What are the higher, transcendental meanings of these groups and their activities?

34. *Patrons, Clients, and Friends* (Cambridge: Cambridge University Press, 1984), 29–42.

35. Ibid., 35.

This structuring into an institutionalized form of exchange takes place through a number of institutional mechanisms and patterns of interaction. Such mechanisms are, for instance, titles or entitlements, hierarchical privileges for the upper classes in traditional societies. Patterns of interactions are, for instance, the gift and hospitality; the form that they take reflects the institutionalized social relationship between the participants. These mechanisms are closely related to the major rituals of the society, which serve to uphold and legitimize the symbols of societal identity and social order. Thus, we see here a combination of social, economic, political, and religious factors, all working together. The institutionalization and the "setting-up" of rules is primarily a work of the elite on the basis of their conceptions and visions. Thus the elite form the predominant cultural orientation in society. The result is a strong element of power and hierarchy in this relationship, although interwoven with long-range solidarity and provision of meaning.

Centralized Economy: Redistribution by a Central Power

The model outlined by Eisenstadt and Roniger is helpful for understanding centralized economic exchange in a society such as that in first-century Palestine. There the Jewish people constituted both the nation and the society, and the temple was the central institution of power. There were criteria for membership, special obligations for members, and differences in goods available for various categories of society, based on sex, age, occupation, and other factors. Moreover, there were hierarchical structures within this society. Finally, the social and economic exchange was embedded in a highly meaningful context of cult and ritual, linking the mundane to the transcendental.

Sahlins explains the close link between the two aspects in this way:

> Redistribution by powers-that-be serves two purposes, either of which may be dominant in a given instance. The practical, logistical function—redistribution—sustains the community or community effort in a material sense. At the same time, or alternatively, it has an instrumental function: as a ritual of communion and subordination to

> central authority, redistribution sustains the corporate structure itself, that is in a social sense. The practical benefits may be critical, but, whatever the practical benefits, chiefly pooling generates the spirit of unity and centricity, codifies the structure, stipulates the centralized organization and social order and social action.[36]

This description of the double effect of redistribution and its embeddedness in the most central aspect of a common culture seems to fit with the interrelation between economy, power, and religion in ancient societies. A central economy of redistribution is well known from temple- or palace-centered economies from the ancient Middle East.[37] It was a way to generate surplus production and to coordinate labor resources: for instance, for large building projects and for strategic use of stockpiled resources.[38]

Redistribution continued as the main socioeconomic system in the Roman republic and empire, but with different types of power structures.[39] One basic form for redistribution was warfare. Although wars were rarely fought for economic reasons,[40] they resulted in a redistribution of wealth: winners in wars confiscated property and labor and redistributed land among soldiers. This practice links the central redistributive system strongly to a reciprocal system in the form of patronage. Military and political leaders needed loyal followers, who were granted land in return for loyalty.

The center of power in the Roman Empire was Rome. Wealth was extracted from the provinces in the form of taxes, either directly through Roman officials and their soldiers or through

36. *Stone Age Economics*, 190.

37. Carney, *The Shape of the Past*, 172–75.

38. Some divide distribution into two sectors: (1) There is genuine redistribution in which goods are collected centrally and redistributed, or (2) there is mobilization in which goods and services are collected into the hands of an elite for their own enterprises, for instance, for the building of monumental buildings. This division seems unwarranted, however, as S. C. Humphreys ("Polanyi," 65) points out that since "the two functions are frequently carried out by the same organisation, and justified in the same way as serving collective interests, the distinction between immediate material distribution and deferred or less measurable benefits of the ruler's activities as priest and warleader does not seem sharp enough to warrant classing 'mobilization' as a separate category." Thus, it seems wise to hold the two sides of redistribution together, one of practical material benefits and one of symbolic, ritual character, but likewise of "real" benefit to the community.

39. Carney, *The Shape of the Past*, 182–86.

40. Finley, *Ancient Economy*, 157.

vassal princes. This wealth was partly used for "conspicuous consumption" by the elites, but some of it was used for broader redistribution, for instance, in the form of large building programs of roads, aqueducts, temples, and fortifications. Everywhere in the Roman Empire the presence of this centralized power in redistribution was clearly felt, but it was forever mixed with patron–client relations.

Patron–Client Relations

From the point of view of this study the patron–client model is particularly relevant, since Eisenstadt and Roniger discuss it as an institution that structures the exchange of goods according to the norms and values of the society at large. That is, we find here a model of an institutionalized form of economic exchange embedded in the social structure.

A few general remarks on how Eisenstadt and Roniger situate their model within the different schools of sociology and social anthropology are in order. They distance their approach from that of the functional school in anthropology and the structural-functional school in sociology. They list the main criticism against this school:

> First, this model—because it assumed a basic social consensus based on central societal values and goals, and because it emphasized the boundary-maintaining mechanisms of social control, and implicitly minimized the importance of power and coercion as a means of social integration—was considered to be unable to explain social conflicts and social change.[41]

A similar criticism has been raised against the use of structural functionalism in sociological studies of the New Testament, notably those of the Jesus Movement, by G. Theissen.[42] Instead of emphasizing the existence of institutions in the functionalist school, new studies focused on the problems of institutions and stressed that institutional structures develop, are maintained, and

41. *Patrons, Clients, and Friends*, 23–24. For the following, see pp. 21–28.

42. John H. Elliott, "Social-Scientific Criticism of the New Testament: More on Methods and Models," *Semeia* 35 (1986): 22–25; R. A. Horsley and J. S. Hanson, *Bandits, Prophets, and Messiahs* (Minneapolis: Winston Press, 1985), xx–xxi.

are changed in a process of interaction and struggle among those who participate in them.

Many of these new approaches in sociology and social anthropology come together in the study of patron–client relations and in the attempt to define their central core. The structural-functional school had focused on groups and their needs and their boundary-maintaining mechanisms. The study of patron–client relations, on the other hand, stressed the "importance of personal and interpersonal relations, quasi-groups, networks and power relations."[43]

Furthermore, this stress on interpersonal relations and exchange was connected with other aspects of social structure and action. First, there was the aspect of the autonomous dynamics of power in society. This led to a stress on the relations between distribution of power, the flow of resources, and the structure of social relations (patron–client), with attention to the hierarchy, asymmetry, and inequality of these relations. Second, the autonomy of the symbolic dimension of human activity and of symbols of transcendental meaning was emphasized. These aspects were seen in the close link between patron–client bonds, ritual kinship, and concepts of honor and other perceptions of social order. Finally, the study of patron–client relations has brought to our attention the problem of continuity or discontinuity in the institutional order.

These aspects of the study of patron–client relations as set forth by Eisenstadt and Roniger make this model very useful for the purpose of this study. It is a model flexible enough to cover a large number of different relationships.

> Patronage is a model or analytical construct which the social scientist applies in order to understand and explain a range of apparent different social relationships: father–son, God–man, saint–devotee, godfather–godchild, lord–vassal, landlord–tenant, politician–voter, professor–assistant, and so forth. All these different sets of social relationships can thus be considered from one particular point of view which may render them comprehensible.[44]

43. Eisenstadt and Roniger, *Patrons, Clients, and Friends*, 27.

44. A. Blok, "Variations in Patronage," *Sociologische Gids* 16 (1969): 366.

Among the chief characteristics of the patron–client relationship, the following are of particular interest for our study:

1. Interaction between patron and client is based on simultaneous exchange of different types of resources. A patron has instrumental, economic, and political resources and can therefore give support and protection. A client, in return, can give promises and expressions of solidarity and loyalty.
2. There is a strong element of solidarity in these relations, linked to personal honor and obligations. There may be a spiritual attachment, however ambivalent, between patrons and clients.
3. Patron–client relations are seemingly binding and long range, ideally of lifelong endurance. But such relations between individuals are in principle entered into voluntarily, and can be abandoned voluntarily.
4. Patron–client relations are based on a very strong element of inequality and difference in power. A patron has a monopoly on certain positions and resources that are of vital importance for his client.

The result is a relationship with a paradoxical combination of elements. Inequality and asymmetry in power are combined with expressions of mutual solidarity in terms of interpersonal sentiments and obligations. Potential coercion and exploitation are combined with voluntary relations and mutual obligations.

Eisenstadt and Roniger have developed their model of patron–client relations within the context of an exchange system based on a central market, that is, a modern economy. In their analysis of the dynamics of the patron–client relations, however, they start with societies in which the clientalistic model is the predominant form of exchange.

PATRON–CLIENT RELATIONS AS A CENTRAL INSTITUTION

Eisenstadt and Roniger distinguish between the various roles that patron–client relations play within the larger social context. In some societies they are part of the central institutional context, as in ancient Rome, southern Europe, Latin America, southeast Asia, and the Middle East. In a second group of societies—for instance, Japan and classical India—they form a recognized part and a legitimate addendum to the institutional context. In a third group, comprising the United States, the Soviet Union, and most democracies, patron–client relations are regarded not as part of, but as an addendum to the institutional center of society.[45] It is the first group of societies that is of interest here.

Most of these societies have an economy based on land, and we recognize the definitions given by Finley of "ancient economy" in the terms used by Eisenstadt and Roniger when they speak of "extensive and extractive economies":

> They aim at expansion of large territories . . . and are characterized by intensive exploitation of a fixed resource basis. Second, these policies are mostly extractive and redistributive ones. In many of these societies and especially in the more centralized ones in the "traditional" periods of their history, the rulers attempted to control the ownership of land either by vesting all the ownership in their own hands or those of fellow aristocrats and making most of the peasant families into tenants of some sort or by supervising and controlling the degree to which the plots of land owned by various kinship units could be transferred freely.[46]

This description of economic policies corresponds largely with the policies pursued by the Romans as well as the Hasmonean and Herodian dynasties in Palestine.

The internal structure of the major social groups was characterized by "internal weakness, evident above all in the relatively low degree of internal solidarity."[47] In Roman society this becomes visible in the ways patrician Romans, generals, and others gathered clients around themselves to gain support in the infighting about power.[48] Supportive relations between members of the ruling class in the form of friendship *(amicitia)* had a similar function.

Another form of patron–client relations was that between Rome and dependent cities, or between prominent Romans and groups

45. Eisenstadt and Roniger, *Patrons, Clients, and Friends*, 50.

46. "Patron–Client Relations as a Model of Structuring Social Exchange," *Comparative Studies in Society and History* 22 (1980): 62.

47. Ibid., 64.

48. Eisenstadt and Roniger, *Patrons, Clients, and Friends*, 55–56. For the following, see pp. 59–64.

of citizens or individuals in Roman-controlled areas. In a way the whole system of Roman administration of controlled areas was characterized by patron–client relations. Thus, the Roman administration of the provinces of the empire fits this general characterization:

> The center impinges on the local (rural, urban or tribal) community mainly in the form of administration of law, the maintenance of peace, exaction of taxation, provision of some distributive goods and the maintenance of cultural and/or religious links to the center . . . but, with few exceptions, most of these links were effected through existing local kinship—territorial and/or ritual—units and subcenters, and/or through patrimonial-like bureaucracies.[49]

This corresponds to Roman rule through vassal princes, such as Herod in Palestine. Similarly on the local level, this form of government does not penetrate the periphery in an independent way.

A. Blok has given a description of a particular form of patronage that develops in such situations: "segmented societies with a central authority which is weak in the countryside, in which patronage may take the form of brokerage or mediation between local communities in the periphery and the urban center."[50] The function of a mediator or a broker is to provide links between two segments of society. Brokers form a channel of communication between the power and culture of the urban centers, in which the values of the elite are formed, and the "little tradition" of villages and peasant culture, which is very much based on older traditions. Thus, brokerage involves a relationship between at least three actors. Vis-à-vis the central authority of the urban elite the broker is a client. With respect to people in the periphery, however, he acts as a patron. Different persons can act as brokers; the broker can be a representative for the central power—for instance, a military commander—or a wealthy landowner in the village, or a "holy man."[51]

49. Eisenstadt and Roniger, "Patron–Client Relations," 65.

50. "Variations in Patronage," 369.

51. P. Brown ("The Rise and Function of the Holy Man in Late Antiquity," *Journal of Roman Studies* 61 [1971]: 87) describes the "holy man" in Syria in the fifth and sixth century C.E. as a broker: "It is precisely at this point that the holy man comes to the fore as a figure in village society and in the relations between the village and the outside world. For what men expected of the holy man coincided with what they sought in the rural patron."

Social relations and economic exchange were linked to symbolic images. Those most clearly related to patron–client relations centered on mediators and various conceptions of honor. There were basic conceptions of cosmic and social order, among which was the conception of tension between a higher transcendental order and the mundane order. But there was little effort to overcome this tension, for instance, by efforts to change society. The reason was the strongly held conception that the cultural and social order was given, so that the perception that one could shape this order through active participation was weak. Moreover, the access to various positions within this order was not free; it was mediated through special groups or ritual experts who represented the "given" order.

What consequences and patterns of interaction did these characteristics generate, according to Eisenstadt and Roniger?

> First of all they tend to develop a low level of societal trust, or rather, the scope of trust that develops in the basic groups of the society is relatively narrow and not easily transferred to broader settings. Second, and closely related, is the fact that this creates a situation in which no category of social actors, above all the higher ones, enjoys any "corporate" legitimation of their attempts to secure their major positions and resources. . . . Third, these characteristics . . . result in a relatively passive definition of identity and trust among the major actors. And fourth, they generate . . . a potential competition between members of each category with respect to their possible access to resources and to the positions that control these resources. All these factors tend to produce a certain pattern of interaction and struggle among members of the same social categories and classes, a pattern characterized by continuous contest, manipulation and perpetual imbalance.[52]

The result of this is a feature that many studies have shown to be prominent in patron–client relations: that they are not stable and continuous, but rather characterized by change and lack of stability.

In many societies there is a criticism of patron–client relations and their channeling of resources, a criticism which often is based on the premise of equality. Efforts to break the system of patronage may take various forms according to the organizational struc-

52. "Patron–Client Relations," 69–70.

ture of a society. In societies in which the clientalistic model of exchange is predominant, however, few such forces for change can develop, and they rarely succeed in changing the pattern.

In societies of this type, protest may take the form of banditry, in which a group of followers gather around a strong leader. The formation of new groups in banditry does not change the basic pattern of society, however; it merely takes away some people from the existing patron–client network. Moreover, the relationship between a rebel leader and his followers frequently resembles that of a patron and his clients.

> The rebel leader may become a rebel patron who "serves" the more downtrodden clients in a given population, but the basic relations between him and his "clients" do not greatly differ from those of the usual patron–client relationships, although there does tend to develop, at least in the initial phases of the struggle, a strong emphasis on the purer interpersonal relationships, as well as on a general communal solidarity between them.[53]

Another example of rebellion against a clientalistic social system is a variant of the first one, and has been documented, for instance, in Brazil. It takes the form of "a new religious leader carrying the message of salvation to the downtrodden. In addition, he restructures or organizes his 'clients' into a new solidary community."[54] This type of rebellion, however, has an equally limited effect upon society, and it does not grant its members access to internal power in this society.

This model of rebellion against a society dominated by patron–client relationships is helpful for understanding the nature of Palestinian politics in the first century C.E. There were several peasant uprisings led by bandits. They are described at length by Josephus, and also mentioned by Luke. The Pharisee Gamaliel sees the Jesus group as being of a type with the uprising by Judah of Galilee (Acts 5:37–39), in that they both represented a challenge to the position of the leading groups in Jerusalem.

According to Eisenstadt and Roniger, one of the characteristics of a society based on patron–client relations was a high degree of instability, imbalance, and contest. This corresponds well with

53. Ibid., 76.
54. Ibid.

analyses of the situation in the Roman Empire in the first century C.E. by Rohrbaugh and Seán Freyne. Rohrbaugh[55] emphasizes the connection between power and wealth. To have wealth without power, that is, without power of one's own or without patrons, meant existing in a precarious situation. But even if one had power one was not totally safe, since there was always some power higher up, as Freyne points out:

> No matter what step of the ladder one had reached there was always someone higher, a situation which made life essentially unstable, if not precarious. Even Antipas could be deprived of his possessions, and benevolence to the deprived does not dominate in such a situation.[56]

We have now laid out the basic pattern of socioeconomic exchange and interaction in a society dominated by patron–client relationships. The primary modes of exchange were reciprocity and redistribution. In contrast to a market exchange, this exchange was not free to follow its own rules; it was embedded in a social and cultural context. Power and social status were important factors that determined the forms of exchange and the outcome for the various actors in this exchange. In particular, the patron–client relationship was an important institution which channeled resources according to power and status.

In the following chapters we shall apply the insights and models from this chapter to Palestine as Luke describes it in his Gospel. Chapter 4 gives a broad picture of this society with special emphasis on the social organization of peasant life and the various forms of reciprocity and redistribution. The model of the patron–client relationship is used to describe the social dynamics at work in Luke's Palestine. Chapter 5 attempts to outline Luke's alternative to the social and economic system that he describes. Modern studies of the economic perspective of peasant societies—"the moral economy of the peasants"—provide a heuristic model to structure the material in Luke. Finally, chapters 6–9 take up the initial question of this study, the role of the Pharisees within this socioeconomic system. The patron–client relationship provides a model within which to understand Luke's picture of the Pharisees.

55. "Social Class," 519–46.

56. *Galilee from Alexander the Great to Hadrian, 323 B.C.E. to 135 C.E.* (Wilmington: Michael Glazier, 1980), 177.

CHAPTER 4

Economic Interaction in Luke's Palestine

Here we shall use the models developed in chapter 3 to outline the social groups and socioeconomic interaction in Palestine as Luke describes it.

Luke viewed the society that he described from various perspectives. In a manner typical of Hellenistic literature he related events in his own narrative to the larger context of events in the Roman Empire. Throughout the Gospel and Acts he links his narrative to historical events or to historical persons, especially to Roman emperors and governors, Jewish kings, princes, and high priests. This was a way to describe the nascent Christian movement as an event of worldwide importance.[1]

The focus of Luke's attention, however, is determined by the history of Jesus and his movements. Thus, in Luke 1—2 the Jerusalem scene with the temple has links with the village scenes of Bethlehem and Nazareth. From Luke 3 through 19:27 the village scene dominates, starting with Jesus' activities in Galilee and with the narrative of his travels through Samaria and Judea as a central piece. Finally, from 19:27 until the end of the Gospel in chapter 24, Jerusalem with her Jewish and Roman authorities is the focus of interest.

These two major scenes, the village periphery and the central city, by and large correspond to the forms of socioeconomic inter-

1. E. Plühmacher, *Lukas als hellenistischer Schriftsteller*, SUNT 9 (Göttingen, W. Ger.: Vandenhoeck & Ruprecht, 1972), 9–31.

action. Reciprocal exchange mostly takes place on the village scene; redistribution and unequal patron–client relationships are connected with the central city. The discussion of Luke's presentation will be divided accordingly in two parts: the village and the city of Jerusalem.

In the discussion of the village scene we shall first present material from the narrative sections about Jesus' travels and actions, and then material from the parables. In this way, both the distinctive character of each type of material and its contribution to a full description of village life become clear. It has been questioned whether one could draw any inferences from descriptions in the parables to the social scene of Palestine. Since we are primarily interested in the typical character of village society rather than the historical question, we will focus on how the parables contribute to the understanding of the social patterns and relationships that Luke presupposes. In fact, this social nature is characteristic of the parables of Jesus.

> Other related forms [proverb, fable, riddle] from the same cultural period take their content from human interpersonal relations and from "nature." But the parables of Jesus are uniformly drawn from the social field of interpersonal relations, with the one exception of the various parables drawn from growing plants.[2]

Parables have been studied for the types of organization and local administration that they reflect,[3] and it has also been suggested that they are a result of a particular stage in the development of division of labor and means of production in Palestine.[4]

THE VILLAGE SCENE

The first part of Jesus' ministry is set in Galilee (4:14—9:50). There follows the travel narrative of the journey to Jerusalem (9:51—19:27). As noted earlier, Jerusalem as the goal for the journey is the main structural element in this narrative, not an

2. W. A. Beardslee, "Parable Interpretation and the World Disclosed by the Parable," *Perspectives in Religious Studies* 3 (1976): 135.

3. A. N. Sherwin-White, *Roman Society and Roman Law in the New Testament* (New York and London: Oxford University Press, 1963), 120–43.

4. H. G. Kippenberg, *Religion und Klassenbildung im antiken Judea*, SUNT 14 (Göttingen, W. Ger.: Vandenhoeck & Ruprecht, 1978), 152–54.

accurate account of Jesus' movements through Galilee, Samaria, and Judea. Although the geographical details are confused, nevertheless the general setting is always peasant towns or villages outside of Jerusalem.

Luke's terminology when referring to these villages is confusing. He does not seem to distinguish between a "town" *(polis)*, which is a technical term for a Hellenistic town with some form of self-government, and a rural "village" *(komē)*. He speaks of Jesus' travels "by city and village" (8:1; 13:22) and he describes villages like Nazareth, Capernaum, Gadara, and Nain as "cities" (2:39; 5:12; 7:11; 8:27).[5] Probably Luke like other New Testament authors uses the term *polis* in a nontechnical sense. This suggestion is supported by the observation that even when Luke speaks of a *polis,* the community that he describes is that of a *komē;* it does not have the institutions of a Hellenistic city, but rather those of a Jewish village.[6]

What is a Village?

"Village" is not only an administrative or economic term for a settlement that is not a "city." As a human community it also has typical social and psychological features. In his classic study *The Little Community: Viewpoints for the Study of Human Whole,*[7] R. Redfield outlines four qualities that characterize "the little community": its distinctiveness, smallness, homogeneity, and all-providing self-sufficiency. These qualities are typical of communities with a simple social structure; when we move up the scale of social complexity these four qualities diminish.

In his study of an Andalusian *pueblo* (village), J. A. Pitt-Rivers reached similar conclusions:

> To sum up, then, the pueblo is a highly centralized community, both structurally and also emotionally. . . . The community is not merely a geographical or political unit, but the unit of society in every context. The pueblo furnishes a completeness of human relations which makes it the prime concept of all social thought.[8]

5. Sherwin-White, *Roman Society*, 129–32.

6. See M. Goodman's *State and Society in Roman Galilee 132–212 A.D.* (Totowa, N.J.: Rowman and Allanheld, 1983), 119–25.

7. (Chicago: University of Chicago Press, 1955), 4.

8. *The People of the Sierra*, 2d ed. (Chicago: University of Chicago Press, 1971), 31–32.

Within the pueblo some are considered members of the village in a full sense whereas others are not. The well-to-do local farmer is a full member, while administrators and small bureaucrats are not; they come from the outside, from the city. Similarly, owners of estates who live part of the year in the city are not regarded as fully part of the village. Likewise, people who have come from other villages or those who have left the pueblo for some reason or other are regarded as "outsiders."

Some of the same features described by Redfield and Pitt-Rivers are found in the villages described by Luke. In his Gospel the villages appear as distinctive and homogeneous entities. Frequently a village is introduced as a unit. On his journeys Jesus meets the population of a village as a whole: "a large crowd" (*ochlos*, 7:11, 12), "all the people *(plēthos)* of the surrounding country of the Gerasenes" (8:37). They form an undifferentiated group; they come together as "the people of the village" or from many villages (8:4), or they are "all in the synagogue" (4:22, 28). Thus, the inhabitants of a village are represented by their village, so that they may even be criticized en bloc, as a unit: "Woe to you, Chorazin, Bethsaida, Capernaum, for if the mighty works done in you had been done in Tyre and Sidon, they would have repented long ago" (10:13).

Since it is the village or the area that is the principal unit, towns and cities outside the area and their inhabitants are looked upon with suspicion. For example, the relations between the Samaritans and the Jews of Galilee and Judea were hostile (9:52–56; 10:25–37; 17:11–19). Skepticism became even stronger when a town or an area was totally foreign, that is, inhabited by non-Jews. That was particularly so with the Phoenician coastal towns of Tyre and Sidon (10:13–14), which had a long history of economic extraction and pressure with the Galilean hinterland. For Jesus to use them as a good example in his woes against Galilean villages thus was bound to provoke outrage. The horizon of the villagers was their village and the nearest surrounding area. The villagers in Capernaum wanted to keep Jesus in their village, but he broke away by pointing to his responsibility for a larger area: "I must preach the good news of the kingdom of God to the other cities also" (4:43).

The People of the Village

When it comes to a closer description of the people of the village, we find different perspectives in the narrative sections and in the parables. In the narratives we meet the large crowds and people at the periphery of the village: the sick, the sinners, and the poor, as well as Jesus and his followers. Village leaders are mostly connected with the synagogue. In the parables the focus is much more on "full" members of the community; we meet a broader variety of people and of leaders. But the pictures that these two parts render are more complementary than contradictory.

On the Village Periphery: The Sick, the Outcast, and the Poor

In his narrative Luke shows special interest in people who stand in a peripheral position to the village community. When Jesus is preaching to large groups, "the crowds," some people are singled out and stand out from the rest. One such group is formed by sick people of various categories. They are either present in the crowd or are brought in by their family or friends (4:40; 5:18–26; 6:17–19; 7:21–22). They were people on the outskirts of the community. They were either temporarily or permanently put in a liminal situation. Some of them suffered from illnesses that made them unclean, such as leprosy (5:12–16; 17:11–19), bleeding (8:43–48), paralysis (13:10–17), or other illnesses (4:40; 6:17–19). Others were possessed by demons (4:33–35; 7:21; 8:26–39). Lumped together with those who suffered from illnesses were the poor *(ptōchoi)*, who were likewise held in low regard in society (7:22; 14:13, 22). These members of the village were not totally cut off from the community; some of the sick apparently were cared for by family and friends.

Other groups seem irrevocably cut off from the rest of the village, especially "sinners," for instance, women who had broken with the purity rules of the community (7:37–39). In this category, regarded as outsiders to the social network of the village, were also toll collectors *(telōnai)* (5:27–32; 15:1–2; 19:1–10). The background for Luke's description of the toll collectors probably was a Galilean system in which indirect taxes were farmed out to individuals on a relatively small scale.[9] Luke presents them not as "traitors" employed by the Romans, but rather as persons who were suspect of dishonesty and apt to misuse their authority.[10]

"Inside" Outsiders: Jesus and His Group

Jesus and his followers are another group who stand out from the larger crowd of the village population. They were part of the village scene, and belonged to the village and to the inside network when they returned to their home villages (4:38–39). Some of the women who followed Jesus had sufficient means to support Jesus and his followers (8:1–3; 10:38–42). At least one of them was of higher status than the ordinary villagers; Joanna was the wife of one of Herod's officials (8:3).

Thus the "inner group" of Jesus' followers apparently were drawn from the village insiders and they kept contact with their families in their own villages. When traveling through other villages, they might, however, have been looked upon with suspicion. And Jesus himself, preacher and healer, was an ambiguous person. On the one hand, he attracted people through his preaching and his healings; on the other hand, he created conflict and formed his own faction. This ambiguity was transformed into a threat when it became apparent that he broke with the long-established norms of the village.

Local Leadership of the Village

Luke does not give a full picture of the leadership of the village, but he introduces some of its representatives. Some of the "elders" *(presbyteroi)* among the Jews in Capernaum are sent by the centurion to act as intermediaries between himself and Jesus (7:1–10). *Presbyteros* could be a honorific title, indicating that this person belonged to the most respected group of men in the village; it could also have the technical meaning of a member of the local town council *(gerousia)*.[11] The term "ruler" *(archōn)* could simi-

9. See Seán Freyne's *Galilee*, 183–94.

10. J. R. Donahue, "Tax Collectors and Sinners," *CBQ* 33 (1971): 58–59.

11. G. Bornkamm, "*presbyteroi*," *TDNT* 6:660.

larly be an indication of honor and status in the community, but it could also be a technical term for a member of a small ruling committee elected from the larger body of the town elders.[12]

The distinction between leadership of the village and of the synagogue is unclear; in many instances, they probably overlapped.[13] No doubt the head of the synagogue council, the *archisynagōgos* (8:41; 13:14), was one of the important leaders of the community. As a representative of minor officials in the synagogue, there is for Luke the synagogue "attendant" (*hyperētes*, 4:20). Most of the terms mentioned so far indicate status and official or unofficial leadership in the village, and no doubt the *presbyteroi* and the *archontes* belonged to the most respected and well-to-do men of the community. So far, Luke's description of village administration seems to go well with what is historically known about Galilee, although most of our information comes from the second century C.E.[14]

It is particularly noteworthy, however, that Luke introduces the Pharisees as belonging to this group of leaders. In one instance, a Pharisee is described as an *archōn* and a rich man (14:1). Furthermore, the Pharisees reside in the villages, show hospitality in their homes (7:36; 11:37), and are present (together with the scribes) to control people's observance of the law (5:17–26, 30–32; 6:6–11; 15:2).

The main concern of the leadership as Luke portrays it is to protect the borders of the village community, both externally and internally. The external borders concerned the relationship between villagers and individuals who had set themselves apart from the community, especially "sinners" and tax collectors, who were considered unclean. Consequently, the villagers are also exhorted not to act in such a way that they themselves become unclean, for instance, by breaking purity laws (6:1–5, 6–11; 13:10–17).

Through the narrative sections of his Gospel, Luke presents a rather one-sided picture of the village community, primarily con-

12. S. Safrai, "Jewish Self-Government," in *The Jewish People in the First Century* 1, ed. S. Safrai and M. Stern (Assen: Van Gorcum, 1976), 414–15.

13. Safrai, "The Synagogue," in *The Jewish People in the First Century* 2:933; Goodman, *Roman Galilee*, 119–23.

14. Goodman, *Roman Galilee*, 119–28.

cerned with the question of boundaries of the community. The village population most of the time is represented by the "crowd" or some such description. Furthermore, we hear little about the social and economic situation, about occupations, or about social relations within the village. Luke gives a clearer picture only of the people at the periphery of this society. They had come into conflict with the norms and values of the community, by illness, poverty, or their own actions. But, since they were marginal, living on the periphery and considered unclean, they represented a danger and a possible source of contamination to the community at large. The leadership of the community, including the Pharisees, was particularly concerned about protecting the community against such outside or inside dangers to the community. Its efforts were concentrated on upholding the purity rules of the community, and in that way keeping the boundaries of the community strong.

Thus, the narrative sections focus very much on Jesus' conflict with community leaders over the boundaries and purity of the community. This probably accounts for Luke's rather one-sided description of village leadership. Luke, for instance, does not mention the leaders' role in overseeing village finances or in public charity.[15] Luke does, however, provide a link to a broader picture of the village leadership in terms of social and economic interaction by portraying at least some of the Pharisees as well-to-do community leaders (14:1–14).

The Village of the Parables

When we move from the narrative sections in Luke to the parables we find a much more vivid description of life in the village.[16] Suddenly the village comes alive, the "crowds" dissolve into individuals, and we get a much clearer picture of social life and economic interaction in the village community. Since so many

15. Ibid., 121–22.

16. In "Characteristics of the Parables in the Several Gospels," *JTS* 19 (1968): 53, M. D. Goulder suggests that the world of Luke's parables is the *town* in contrast to the *village*. We are here speaking, however, of a preindustrial situation in which towns are *peasant towns,* linked to the countryside and dependent upon farming. Therefore, the examples that Goulder gives do not so much show a contrast between a town and a village as a contrast between Luke's focus on human relationships and the nature parables typical of Mark.

of the parables are found among the Gospels in Luke only, it may be justified to speak of a Lukan village scene as illustrated by parables such as "the Good Samaritan" (10:29–37); "the importunate friend at midnight" (11:5–8); "the rich fool" (12:16–21); "on invitation of guests" (14:16–24); "the lost sheep and the lost coin" (15:3–10); "the prodigal son" (15:11–32); "the rich man and Lazarus" (16:19–31); and "the unjust judge" (18:1–8).

We recognize the village community with its various groups from the narrative section, but there is a considerable shift in emphasis. The narrative section focused on people in a marginal position and the role of a village leadership concerned with matters of purity and community boundaries. The parables, however, most frequently focus on full members of the community, for instance, peasants, and on their social and economic interactions.

Furthermore, the world presented through the parables is an exaggerated world: the rich are very rich and the poor are extremely poor. This is particularly striking when the two groups are juxtaposed, as with the rich man and Lazarus in 16:19–31. But in comparison with Matthew, the economy of Luke's parables is rather modest; for instance, when he speaks of debts, the sums involved are small compared to Matthew's fantastic figures (Luke 7:41–42; Matt. 18:23–25).[17] Moreover, viewed against the background of known differences between the very rich and the poor in the Greco-Roman world at this period, the differences in Luke's parables are rather down to earth.[18] Maybe this reflects the origin of the parables in a small-scale economy; their perspective is that of a peasant economy that depicts the world of the rich as an enlargement of their own world, within imaginable quantities. Thus, it has been suggested that this points to a Galilean origin for the parables.[19]

The Village Population in the Parables: Differences between Insiders

In the parables, the inhabitants of the village span from the very rich to the very poor. On the top there is the rich man in the

17. Goulder, "Characteristics of the Parables," 54–55.

18. See Richard Duncan-Jones's *The Economy of the Roman Empire* (Cambridge: Cambridge University Press, 1982), 343–44, 17–32.

19. Sherwin-White, *Roman Society*, 139–41.

parable of the rich man and Lazarus (16:19–31). The description of him as one who "was clothed in purple and fine linen and feasted sumptuously every day" (16:19) is quite similar to that of the king's courtiers in 7:25. He is seen as belonging more to the "outside" rich than to the village in a full sense, and by his unwillingness to help Lazarus he had put himself outside the village community. On the very top is also the "man" (not "king," as in Matt. 22:1–10) in 14:16–24 who sent out invitations to a great banquet, only to receive excuses from his guests, apparently also themselves people with property consisting of land and cattle.

Our use of models from economies of peasant and ancient societies based on land appear well founded. Wealth in the village community of Luke's parables comes from land, and the rich men are owners of land, fruit farms, and cattle. Landowners who had several farms, orchards, and vineyards could lease them out to tenants (20:9–16). Other large landowners lived on their own land and took part in the work of the land; this must have been the case with the rich fool (12:16–21) and the father with two sons (15:11–32).

One step down in wealth and status we find a large group of peasants and tenants. Peasants are smallholders who own a small piece of land and who work it themselves together with their family and perhaps with some hired help. In this group we probably find the sower in his field (8:4–8), the man in bed with his children (11:5–8), and the woman with the ten silver coins (15:8–10). The difference between peasants who owned their own land and others who were tenants (16:1–9; 20:9–16) was not necessarily a large one.[20] The most important factor was not that of formal legal status, but the question of their dependence upon others and their right to dispose of their income. The designation of individuals as "debtors" (7:41–42) reveals their dependent status; they did not have the right to the produce from the land they were working, but were subordinate to a landlord or patron.

The next group actually consists of several groups: dependent workers, servants, and slaves. This was not a consistent group or one easy to place socially. Some "servants" in the service of a rich man might be highly trusted stewards *(oikonomoi),* in charge of

20. See Freyne's *Galilee,* 165–66.

their master's property while he was away, either temporarily or permanently, as absentee landlords. Most of the "servants" and "slaves" *(douloi, paides)* were house-servants or workers in the fields (12:35–38; 14:17–22; 15:26; 17:7–10). In a similar category, but in an even more insecure position, was the "landless proletariat," day laborers without any security for work or income (10:2; 15:17; 16:3). Also in a precarious situation were widows (18:2–5), beggars (16:3), and the bands of the poor, the maimed, the lame, and the blind (14:13). Here we find a link to Luke's interest in the marginal people in the narrative parts. Finally, there are the outsiders who have left the village and taken to robbery (10:30).

Local Leadership

In the parables, the most prominent representative of the local leadership is the judge (*kritēs,* 12:58; 18:2). This was a general leadership role in the community.[21] Josephus describes judges in a similar way, as local leaders who also serve as mediators between country people and central authorities.[22] Priests, Levites, and Pharisees are mentioned (10:29–37; 18:9–14), but they do not occupy important positions. One minor village official is mentioned: the "servant of law" *(practōr),* who was assigned to assist the judge (12:58). Maybe tax collectors are to be included here; but Luke consistently describes them not from the point of view of their function, but from the point of view of popular opinion of them.

The Village and the Outside World

It is part of Luke's literary style to link the events of his narrative to the larger scene of Roman history. That is primarily information for his readers, however; on the village scene itself, the outside world seems very distant. Jerusalem is the goal for Jesus' journey, and the leaders there often loom in the background. At one point Pharisees and teachers of law from Jerusalem are among those who have come to check on him (5:17); another time Jesus refers to the Jewish leadership in Jerusalem as a threat to his life (9:22).

21. Goodman, *Roman Galilee,* 122–23.
22. Freyne, *Galilee,* 198.

The references to the immediate power-holder of the area, Herod Antipas, the tetrarch of Galilee, have a similar function. Several times he is mentioned almost as a bad omen. First, he is connected with the death of John the Baptist (3:19–20); second, he is said to be eager to see a sign from Jesus at the beginning of Jesus' career (9:7–9); and finally, a group of Pharisees tells Jesus that Herod is searching for him to kill him (13:31–33). These passages prepare Luke's readers for the role Herod plays in the trial of Jesus. They also serve to inform that the activities of Jesus, traveling the villages of Galilee with his disciples and gathering large crowds of people, did not go unnoticed by the political powers of the region. There even was some involvement from this group among the followers of Jesus: Joanna, one of the women who followed Jesus, was the wife of one of Herod's high officials (8:3). Pilate and his execution of a number of Galileans (13:1) also are mentioned; this incident, too, serves to link the narrative about Jesus on the village circuit to the powers outside of that scene.

This world outside of the village is seen from afar, however, and it is culturally miles apart. The perception of what life at Herod's court was like clearly shows that it is seen from the perspective of simple life in a village. It comes through in Jesus' question to the crowds about John the Baptist: "What did you go out to see? A man clothed in soft clothing? Behold, those who are gorgeously appareled and live in luxury are in kings' courts" (7:25).

The outside world and its central powers nonetheless had local representatives in the village. Soldiers were stationed there, and in one instance we hear of the important role of a centurion in Capernaum (7:1–10). He is clearly an outsider in the village, both because he represents the outside administrative and military power and because he is a non-Jew. Obviously, however, he had taken upon himself the function of a patron to the town; expenses for a synagogue were one example of the benefits that he bestowed upon the townspeople. His position probably also implied that he served as a mediator between the local area and central authorities. His patronage implied the function of brokerage. In return, the local leaders of the town, who were his clients, could perform a service by establishing contact with Jesus and asking him to heal the centurion's servant. In this they served as mediators and brokers between the powerful benefactor of their village and Jesus, an even more powerful benefactor.

The narrative sections focus mostly on the administrative and military outside powers. The parables confirm this picture, and also show their linkage with the outside economic powers that most directly affected life of the villagers in terms of their livelihood. We hear about a "nobleman" *(eugenēs)* who went abroad to establish his kingdom (19:12–27), apparently a reference to the various princes of the Herodian family who had obtained the status of vassal kings from the Roman emperor.[23] Before he left he gave out money to his servants *(douloi)* for them to trade with. These "servants" were not ordinary house slaves, but rather trusted associates who were dependent upon the prince. The rewards that they receive upon the return of their master makes this clear: they are given authority over five or ten "cities" (19:17, 19). This authority probably was that of a commander of a toparchy, an administrative unit comprising several villages and the areas around them.[24]

On a smaller scale, there is the absentee landlord with tenants who owed him large sums (16:1–9). This landlord had a steward, a manager *(oikonomos)* who was not a house slave (as in 12:41–48) but rather a free agent with considerable authority on behalf of his master and who conducted business with his master's tenants.

To sum up, the parables more clearly show the dependent relationship of the villagers vis-à-vis a central administration and absentee landlords. Thus, the village population stand in a dependent relationship to a lord or a patron of some sort, be it the ethnarch, the absentee landlord, or a rich landowner in the village. This lord usually acts through an intermediary, a commander or agent, who may act as a broker in this relationship.

RECIPROCAL RELATIONSHIPS IN THE VILLAGE

Among members of the village, social and economic relations are characterized by reciprocal exchange, as outlined in the preceding chapter. That implied the presentation or exchange of "food

23. Fitzmyer, *Luke (X–XXIV)*, 1234–35. These "political" motifs are not found in the parallel story in Matt. 25:14–30.

24. Sherwin-White, *Roman Society*, 127.

and other gifts, labor and hospitality" which takes place between "affinal groups or between neighbours."[25] But we also find the lopsided exchange characterized by large inequalities in power in patron–client relationships between dependent peasants and landlords. Since the latter frequently are absentee landlords, this exchange moves toward the central economy of redistribution, which will be treated in the next section.

Family Units

The family is the most immediate relationship between people. Luke takes this for granted, but there are a number of aspects about family life that he does not consider. Compared to Paul's letters, there is little mention of emotions and sexuality. Luke's focus is upon the family as a social unit in the village, in every aspect a basic unit for its members. Therefore, most activities that he relates are concerned with pooling of resources in terms of sharing food, other possessions, and labor.[26] It is in this sharing that the relationship between family members finds its primary expression. Moreover, this emphasis shows that Luke depicts a small peasant economy in which family members are dependent upon each other for the upkeep of life.

Children are dependent upon their parents (fathers) for the necessities of life (11:11–13). A widow is totally dependent upon her only son (7:11–17). Two sisters who share a house together also are supposed to share the work (10:38–42). Brothers are part of the extended family with whom one would normally share hospitality (14:12). A son is the heir to his father's property, but as long as his father lives the son is supposed to share work on the land and to be obedient (15:29; 20:13–15). For a son to claim his share of the inheritance while his father is still alive is a challenge to his father's authority, as well as an upset of the family economy.[27] After the death of the father, of course, a division of the inheritance would be the normal procedure, but one that frequently caused conflicts between brothers (12:13).

25. Humphreys, "Polanyi," 65.

26. Similar to primitive economy; see Sahlins's *Stone Age Economics*, 94.

27. K. E. Bailey, *Poet and Peasant: A Literary Cultural Approach to the Parables in Luke* (Grand Rapids: Wm. B. Eerdmans, 1976), 161–68.

Neighbors, Friends, and Partners

Villagers who worked the same trade might enter into structured partnerships with fixed obligations to share work, expenditure, and income. Simon Peter, James, and John were partners *(koinōnoi)* in fishing on the Sea of Gennesaret (5:1–11). Fishing could be organized in another way, as Mark relates in his version of the story (1:16–20): James and John were fishermen with their father, Zebedee, who also hired day laborers *(misthōtoi)* in his boat.[28] In 5:29 we hear of a party in the house of Levi, the tax collector, who had invited a group of other tax collectors; possibly this group of colleagues made up a guild.

Friendship was a relationship that was less structured and less formal. It carried many obligations, but first and foremost the moral obligation to help a friend when he was in need. In order to be an honorable man one must fulfill one's obligations to one's friends. On the other hand, one ought not to put excessive demands upon them (11:5–8).[29] Within the bonds of friendship sharing hospitality was normal and to be expected (11:5–8; 14:12; 15:6, 9).

People in a village lived so close that if only for practical reasons it was important to have a good relationship with one's neighbors. Several parables concentrate upon the sharing aspect of this relationship. Neighbors were invited to share a banquet and were expected to reciprocate by inviting in turn (14:12). Villagers of modest means would likewise invite their neighbors to share their celebrations, be it over the return of a lost sheep or a lost coin (15:6, 9).

Master–Servants, Landowner–Tenants, Patron–Clients

Most of the relationships on the village scene are between unequal partners. They cover a wide variety and sometimes several types are found within the same story. In a number of cases the terminology used focuses on the economic aspect of this relationship between unequal partners: for instance, "lender"

28. W. H. Wuellner, *The Meaning of "Fishers of Men"* (Philadelphia: Westminster Press, 1967), 60–61.

29. Bailey, *Poet and Peasant*, 119–33.

(danistēs) and "debtor" *(chreopheiletēs),* "lord" *(kyrios)* and "debtor" (7:41; cf. 6:34; 16:5), "father" (i.e., "landowner") and "day laborer" (*misthios,* 15:17).

One form of such an unequal relationship is that between a master and his servants or slaves on the land or in the house. They might be trusted servants who acted as messengers on his behalf (14:17–24; 20:9–19). Between an absentee landlord and his ordinary servants there was a more distant relationship; in this case, however, another person enters. He is the steward *(oikonomos)* who is in charge of the house while his master is away (12:41–48). In this parable, the steward is an important figure, and Luke focuses on the triangular relationship between the persons involved. The steward has a middle position and is answerable to his master for his arrangement of the house, in particular, for his dealings with the other servants.

Similarly in the landlord–tenant relationship there is the middleman, who serves as an agent between the landlord and his tenants. The steward *(oikonomos)* in the parable in 16:1–9 probably was a free agent who acted independently on behalf of the landowner.[30] It was primarily the large absentee landowners who needed agents. The owner of the vineyard in the parable in 20:9–19 lives close enough to deal with his tenants directly through a servant messenger *(doulos),* who could not act independently of his master.

Likewise in a middle position, this time between a prince or a tetrarch and the village population in an area, were the servants *(douloi)* who served as commanders of the area (19:12–27). Since the Herodian vassal kings and tetrarchs, who probably serve as model for the "prince" in this parable, were also large landowners, the relationship between the prince and the villagers, mediated through the "servants," covered not only administrative but also economic aspects. It was a patron–client relationship in its broadest sense.

The landlord–tenant or agent–tenant relationship was not only a lopsided economic arrangement but also covered a much wider area of social interactions and obligations. Rich landlords were

30. See below, p. 140.

patrons who carried responsibilities for their clients: for example, by giving their tenants loans in a bad year (16:1–9; 7:41–42). An agent might also conduct his business with tenants in such a way as to incur gratitude and compensation in some form in return (16:4–8). Social relations in the narrative section function within the same pattern: the centurion in Capernaum who built a synagogue for the village acted as patron and was repaid by the recognition and assistance of the elders in the village (7:4–5). Hospitality was one way in which the rich provided for their clients and friends. At the same time, it served to incur gratitude and to build support for the rich and to gain authority in the village (14:7–14; 15:22–24).[31]

MONEY AND MARKET IN THE LUKAN VILLAGE

Reciprocal exchange between equals or between patrons and clients was the predominant form of exchange within the village. But what was the role of market exchange and money in this society? The definition of market exchange by S. C. Humphreys is that it "makes transactions possible between individuals irrespective of their social relationship."[32] What are the examples of this kind of exchange in Luke's Gospel? In his outline of peasant economy, M. Nash emphasized as a typical feature the "absence of money as *the* medium of exchange."[33] Therefore, we shall raise questions: How much was money used? What was "money" in the Palestinian village that Luke describes, and what was it used for? And finally, how did peasants get their money?

Market Exchange

Market exchange can play an important part in peasant economy. We find evidence for that in sources that do not deal with economy as such. For instance, in Norwegian fairy tales we find as a popular motif the story of a man who goes to the market to sell or to buy, often through barter, and who ends up by making a fool of

31. For hospitality as a means to gain status, see J. R. Gregory's "Image of Limited Good, or Expectations of Reciprocity," *Current Anthropology* 16 (1975): 78.

32. "Polanyi," 65.

33. "The Organization of Economic Life," 6.

himself. His business turns out to be a failure. Nevertheless, he is received by his loving wife as a hero. This part of the story is not so important to us; the interesting aspect is what light these fairy tales throw upon the market as an important place for trade and exchange in a peasant economy.

Luke does not give direct information about market exchange in the form of descriptions of market scenes. When he describes "the market" *(agora)* it is not as a trade center or a place of exchange (the "commercial *agora*" in Hellenistic towns); rather, it is the "civic *agora,*" the arena for social life and gatherings of people.[34] It is here that children play (7:32) and that prominent people of the community meet, greeted with respect by other villagers (11:43; 20:46). Luke's narrative focuses on the *agora* as an important center for the civic life of a community.[35]

Therefore, it is not through descriptions of a commercial market, but rather more indirectly that Luke gives witness to the existence of a market exchange. One such way is through his use of terms for "buy" *(agorazō)* and "sell" *(pōleō),* which, when they are used together, indicate market exchange as a part of the total social exchange within the village. One example is a passage unique to Luke: "Likewise, as it was in the days of Lot—they ate, they drank, they bought, they sold, they planted, they built, . . . so it will be on the day when the Son of man is revealed" (17:28–30).[36] "Buy" and "sell" are used together also in 22:36: "Let him who has no sword sell his mantle and buy one." The idea here is obviously not to exchange goods through barter, but rather to sell one item and buy another one. Luke points to the need for money in these exchanges, for instance, in terms of carrying a purse (22:36).[37] In

34. On the distinction between the "commercial *agora*" and the "free *agora*," free of all merchandise, see M. M. Austin and P. Vidal-Naquet, *Economic and Social History of Ancient Greece: An Introduction* (Berkeley and Los Angeles: University of California Press, 1980), 377–80.

35. S. B. Hoenig, "The Ancient City-Square: The Forerunner of the Synagogue," in *Aufstieg und Niedergang der römischen Welt* II (19:1, Principat: Religion), ed. W. Haase (Berlin: Walter de Gruyter, 1979), 448–54.

36. The description of the days of Noah in 17:27, which is from Q (Matt. 24:38–39), does not mention these examples of "economic exchange." Note also Luke's adding of "lending money" to the description of human activities in 6:32–36, likewise from the Q source (Matt. 5:43–47).

37. Not carrying a purse thus means to place oneself outside of this society (10:4; cf. 12:33).

one instance, the price for a purchase is given (12:6). In most instances, however, when Luke speaks of buying and selling, he is not concerned with the medium of exchange or the price, but rather the object that is obtained: a field, five yoke of oxen (14:18–19), food (9:13). To sell one's possessions was also one way to obey the commands of Jesus to give to the needy (12:33; 18:22).

In most instances Luke uses terms for "sell" and "buy" that appear to presuppose money as the medium of exchange. These passages give little indication, however, of the relative importance of this type of exchange compared to other forms. Several of these texts do not deal with ordinary daily life in the village, but prescribe a mode of action for those who will break away from their homes and leave the village to become followers of Jesus (12:33; 18:22; 22:36). Does this imply that "buying" and "selling" were more important for those who were not totally embedded in the village, but who were traveling? Or could it even be an inference of a city economy, where the market held a prominent position?

Money as a Medium of Exchange

What was the money used in Luke's village society? Starting with the smallest currency, the smallest copper coin mentioned is a *lepton* (12:59; 21:2). A *lepton* was the smallest copper coin minted by the Jewish tetrarchs, its value only one-eighth that of the other copper coin, the *assarion.* Two *assarions* are mentioned as the price of five sparrows (12:6). The *assarion,* in its turn, was one-sixth of the *dēnarion,* a silver coin in value equivalent to the daily wage of a laborer. The copper coins are mentioned in passages that emphasize the poverty of their owner or the insignificant sum that they represent. Thus, they appear to be money for small transactions among poor villagers. But they were the only coins that the Jewish tetrarchs had the privilege to mint themselves, and therefore they were of some importance.

The *dēnarion,* a silver coin, was minted in Rome. This coin, which carried the image and inscription of the emperor, is at the center of one of the most famous discussions of money in the New Testament, the question of the tribute to Caesar. Two *dēnarii* was the sum paid by the Samaritan to the innkeeper for the care of the man who had fallen among robbers (10:35). In another parable, five hundred and fifty *dēnarii* are mentioned as examples of a large and a small debt (7:41–42). The *drachmē* is a Greek silver coin; its value was equivalent to that of the *dēnarion*. Ten drachmas represented a small savings for a woman (15:8).

Luke also mentions a different kind of money from the older system of fixed quantities based on weight. Thus, "silver" *(argyrion)* carries the meaning of "money" (9:3; 22:5). The "pounds" that are mentioned in the parable of the nobleman and his servants are *minas*, a Greek weight unit for silver, in value about one hundred *dēnarii*. Thus the sum given to each amounted to about one thousand *dēnarii*.[38]

In addition to trade in money, Luke also tells of trade in kind. This form for exchange is an example not of a market economy, but exchange within patron–client relationships or within the system of central redistribution. Tenants of a vineyard paid a percentage of the crop in lease (20:10). Similarly with the tenants of fields, their "loans" of one hundred baths of oil and one hundred cors of wheat most likely were the rent agreed upon (16:6–7).[39] These were large sums and consequently implied the lease of a large plot of land. Other exchanges in kind included tithes to the temple (11:42; 18:12). Luke frequently mentions tax collectors, but he does not explicitly say whether customs and taxes were paid in money or in kind.

To sum up our findings, we must say that market economy as such does not play an important role in this society described by Luke. Except for the example from the court of a prince (19:12–27), the objects of trade are either small or related to local agriculture. Thus, even exaggerated sums in the parables are modest, reflecting a small-scale peasant economy.

Although the market exchange as such does not figure prominently in Luke's Gospel, money in the form of coins or silver pieces appears as a much-used medium of exchange. But this is an ex-

38. Again Luke's economy is on a much smaller scale than that of Matthew, who speaks of one, two, and five talents (25:14–30). One talent was sixty *minas*; thus, five talents amounted to thirty thousand *denarii.*

39. For the various categories of tenants and rental systems in use, see S. Applebaum's "Economic Life in Palestine," in *The Jewish People in the First Century* 2, ed. S. Safrai and M. Stern (Assen: Van Gorcum, 1976), 659–60.

change not so much in form of trade at a "free market" as in the form of obligations from the peasants towards their superiors. These obligations included debts and rents to landlords for the lease of land, taxes and customs to the Roman administration, and offerings to the temple. Thus, in the passages referring to money we do not enter the social world of traders and business people, but that of the peasant. When Luke mentions money and monetary transactions, he may be describing the transition from a peasant economy based on exchange of goods to a monetary economy, though not a free-market one. The peasants got the money to meet their obligations by selling the surplus of their production. The prices for the produce of the smallholders were not set by a "free" market, but were determined by large landowners. Thus, the demand to pay taxes and rent in money was another way to increase the pressure upon smallholders and to make them more dependent upon larger landlords.[40]

JERUSALEM AND THE CENTRAL POWER STRUCTURE

With Jesus' entry into Jerusalem (19:28–40), the scene of Luke's Gospel changes. Jerusalem is the goal for Jesus' journey as the city of God's temple and the center of divine and human power in Palestine. Thus Jesus moves from the village periphery to the central city, which is the scene for the rest of Luke's narrative.

In one important respect the situation is similar to that in the village scenes of the narrative sections in the first part of the Gospel. Luke's focus is again upon Jesus' conflict with the elite, the leaders, while the people, here the "urban nonelite," stand at the side and are largely undifferentiated; they are "the people" (*laos*, 20:1, 9, 45; 22:2; 23:27). The most important single group that is mentioned is made up of the women who followed Jesus (23:27, 49, 55). Otherwise, individuals are only singled out when they are needed for the narrative of Jesus, as representatives of the ordinary, "small" people of the city (19:33; 21:1–4; 22:10–13, 56; 23:39–43). There is a growing tension between the people and the

40. Kippenberg, *Klassenbildung*, 51–53.

leadership, climaxing in the contrasting reactions to the death of Jesus (23:35).

Luke's description of Jewish leaders is determined by the conflict between them and Jesus. The leadership is frequently spoken of as consisting of the groups that made up the Sanhedrin: the chief priests and the scribes together with the elders (that is, the Sadducean priestly families, professional interpreters of the Torah, and the lay nobility consisting of big landowners living in Jerusalem). Luke is not consistent in his terminology when referring to these various groups, but one group is always mentioned: the chief priests (20:1; 22:66; 23:4, 13). This emphasis upon the chief priests highlights the fact that this leadership is centered around the temple, the predominant national institution of power (19:45–47; 21:5–9, 20–21; 23:45; 24:53). There is little mention of the Pharisees and the Sadducees as groups (19:39; 20:27–38), probably because of this emphasis upon the official character of the leadership as connected with the main institutions of power, the temple and the Sanhedrin.

At their disposal the leaders of Jerusalem had a number of subordinates of various kinds: officers and officials (22:50, 52), clients, and dependent followers, who represented the "popular support" for their policies (20:20; 23:4–5, 20–23). The crowds *(ochlos)* or the people *(laos)* have no independent role in the case against Jesus, and whenever possible, Luke emphasizes that the leaders carry the responsibility (22:2; 23:26–27, 35).

The Roman administration occupies a central role in the Jerusalem narrative. The ever-present Roman claim to subservience surfaces in the question about the tribute to Caesar (20:20–26). Roman rule is carried out by Pontius Pilate, the procurator, and his soldiers (Luke 23). The charges that are brought against Jesus accuse him of directly attacking Roman authority by setting himself up as a king (23:2). Luke is eager to point out that Pilate finds the charges false, however; within Luke's scenario they emphasize the combination of political, religious, and economic factors involved in the struggle over authority and leadership over the Jewish people.

Herod, the tetrarch of Galilee, reappears in Jerusalem. In this way, the power "behind the scenes" in Galilee links that part of Luke's narrative directly to Jerusalem. In one of his "asides," explanatory comments to his readers, Luke makes an interesting comment upon the relationship between Pilate and Herod (23:12). They had been enemies, rivals over power, but in their dealings with Jesus they became friends *(philoi)*. This is not just a description of a state of emotions; the ancient institution of friendship plays a dominant role in Luke's Gospel,[41] and the model here apparently is the *amicitia*,[42] a term for an alliance of mutual interest between equals, usually of high status: for instance, Roman nobles. The main purpose was to promote their interests of various kinds, but the alliance also had at its core a moral element of trust.

The Central Authority and the System of Redistribution

In the first nineteen chapters of Luke's Gospel, most references to economic exchange were to the reciprocal exchange between villagers or between tenants and landlords. This last form of lopsided reciprocity between unequals in a patron–client relationship, as well as the system of taxes and customs that is mentioned, points to the central powers in the country. On the village scene these powers are far away; in the Jerusalem section of the Gospel they are on center stage. This is where the power is.

In the first part of the passion narrative there is a concentration of references to money and economic interaction. First comes the expulsion of vendors from the temple (19:45–46); next, the question about tribute to Caesar (20:20–26); and finally, the widow's gift to the temple treasury (21:1–4). These instances are all related to the system of redistribution through a central authority. The authority that Jesus challenges in these narratives is the power to control the collection and redistribution of resources belonging to the Jewish people.

The selling in the temple court was linked directly to sacrifices in

41. Luke uses *philos* fifteen times, Matthew once, and Mark never. Cf. the Hellenistic notion that "friends have all in common" as a background for Acts 2:45–47 and 4:34–35.

42. Eisenstadt and Roniger, *Patrons, Clients, and Friends,* 61–62.

the temple, a main source of income for the temple, and the offerings to the temple treasury that were meant for redistribution among the poor. This corresponds to the two main aspects of redistribution mentioned by Humphreys:

> The two functions are frequently carried out by the same organization, and justified in the same way as serving collective interests, . . . [the] immediate material distribution and the deferred or less measurable benefits of the ruler's activities as priest or warleader.[43]

In this case the "less measurable benefits" were "politico-religious": the temple liturgy guaranteed the security of the people in their relationship with God. Thus, the central collection of resources through tithes, offerings, and such has the cult as its rationale and ultimate goal, and it is regarded by most Jews "as satisfying the basic unit's need for service and goods which it cannot produce alone."[44]

None of this appears to be criticized by Luke, who holds the temple as such in high regard. His criticism focuses on another element of this system of central redistribution: the use of these resources by the central leadership for their own selfish purposes. Tithes are not mentioned in this part of the Gospel (11:42; 18:12), but they were also a part of the central collection, justified through a system of loyalty and obligations. Thus, the power and authority of the temple leadership was expressed also in its control of people's resources. Through a system of taxes, tithes, and sacrifices, it exercised control over the Jewish nation. Another aspect of this control that goes unmentioned by Luke, however, is the role of the temple as a large landowner.

The tax to Rome similarly expressed a claim to subjection and was a mark of Roman control over conquered nations. It is from this perspective that the tax to Caesar is discussed (20:20–26), as well as the accusation that Jesus forbade people to pay this tribute (23:2). This is another indication of how the economy was embedded in society; a major factor of the tax was its expression of a claim to power and honor, thus linking the economic to the political and the social. Customs, another important form of collection

43. "Polanyi," 65.
44. Ibid.

and redistribution (3:13; 19:1–10), is also mentioned in the same terms as the tribute to Caesar—in personal, rather than institutional terms—and it is people, not the system, who are criticized. This observation of Luke's language corresponds with some remarks by T. F. Carney on the effects of a lack of categories for economic theory in antiquity.

> Hence discussion of economic matters was, manifestly, not easy in antiquity. Confronted with governmental tax demands which inevitably meant economic ruin, a taxpayer could not argue out the adverse long-term economic consequences. He could only talk about personalities, on ethical grounds.[45]

Probably the central system of redistribution was not perceived as much different from that of reciprocal exchange between individuals. Within both systems the villagers were confronted with dues to their lords, be they landlords, the prince, or the Roman emperor. Therefore, the protest was raised in personal terms; it was the individual or the group that exploited them who was to blame. The system of divisions between lords and laborers was not questioned. Thus the only possible expression of protest within this framework had to be couched in personal categories and in power language. The unjust landlord or even the emperor was not the highest power; there was one power still higher up, over them, and that was God. The Roman emperor did not have the right to an exclusive claim of lordship; that was a privilege of God alone. God was the ultimate power, and he was the patron and benefactor of the low and needy. Therefore, the power of the unjust lord or even the emperor would be brought down.

CONCLUSION: THE DYNAMICS OF PALESTINIAN PEASANT SOCIETY

We have now outlined the basic structure of socioeconomic organization and interaction in Palestine as Luke describes it. Now we want to sum up our findings. What were the forces and dynamics at work within this society, and what were the relations between various groups? Luke clearly envisages a hierarchical society, which can be illustrated thus:

45. *The Shape of the Past,* 213–14.

1. The emperor.
2. Rulers in Palestine and Syria: (A) Roman consuls/procurator. (B) Tetrarchs (Herodian "kings").
3. High priests and Jerusalem aristocracy, large landowners.
4. The subordinates of (2) and (3): officers and officials, agents in local areas of Palestine.
5. Village leaders: Rich farmers, synagogue leaders, Pharisees.
6. Peasants, "full" members of the village.
7. Village "outsiders": Deviants, unclean, sinners, tax collectors, needy.

This is a top-heavy structure in terms of power; in terms of population, most people are in the bottom categories. Since power was so unevenly distributed, there was a heavy pressure from the top upon the village population. They were in a position of crisis. This is indicated by the high number of instances where Luke speaks of debts and loans. In addition to 12:58–59, which has a parallel in Matt. 5:25–26, there are three other passages that are uniquely Lukan (6:34; 7:41–42; 16:1–9). They refer to a situation of large debts as a well-known fact, and the reduction or outright forgiveness of debts is recounted as totally unexpected, as an "otherworldly" way of acting.

Being in debt put the villagers in a very vulnerable position vis-à-vis their creditors, that is, their landlords or rich landowners. Several parables give clear indications both of the precarious situation of tenants and of the built-up antagonism and criticism against the landlords (16:1–8; 19:12–27; 20:9–16). The parable in 19:12–27 of the "nobleman" who went to a faraway country to become king against the will of his people, and his "servants" who ruled villages, is a telling example. Here Luke links the estate owners with the rule of "kings," in his Gospel typified by Herod, who is roundly denounced for "all the evil things" that he had done (3:19).

No wonder, then, that the housemaster and the agent in charge of the estate of the absentee landlord became important figures. They were local representatives of the distant power, middlemen or brokers to whom tenants and servants could look for help. But there was also the danger that they would enrich themselves at the cost of those under them. The same danger was present in the case of the "middle level" of administration represented by officers with their soldiers. An officer could serve as patron and broker for a village (7:1–10). The presence of armies in the countryside, Roman as well as Herodian, however, added to the pressure put upon them. This is reflected in the charge by John the Baptist to soldiers: "Rob no one by violence or by false accusations" (3:14). The line between rule by legitimate rulers and plunder by robbers, another element that made the countryside insecure (3:14; 6:29; 10:29–37; 11:21–22), could become thin.

Moreover, this crisis in the village society is attested by the way in which Luke speaks of God as benefactor. A prominent aspect of the picture of God is that he will undertake an extreme redistribution of goods, and redirect the flow of resources from the rich to the needy (1:52–53; 6:20–26).

The various claims upon the villagers seem to be interrelated: that of the patron–client relationship, of the temple with its demands of loyalty, and of the Romans, supported by military power. In Luke's presentation and underlying the parables, there appears to be a strong resentment particularly against the large landowners and the ethnarch, Herod. It is in this direction the popular hostility seems to be directed, while the Romans do not seem to receive such hostile opposition. Furthermore, Luke appears to distinguish between the temple cult as a center for God's presence and the leaders who control the temple. The temple aristocracy is criticized. Similarly, on the local level of the village, Luke apparently has a high regard for the law, but criticizes the Pharisees who were the interpreters of the law. Thus, temple and Torah are revered by Luke, but those who were in authority over the temple or over the interpretation of the Torah are criticized as part of the oppression of the people.

Next we turn to the question of the basis for Luke's criticism. What was his alternative to a control of resources by the elite?

CHAPTER 5

Luke's Perspective: The Moral Economy of the Peasant

What was Luke's alternative to the economic exchange governed by the power of the elites? What was the system that he advocated? A return to the teachings of the prophets? Certainly, Luke very much based his teaching on expositions of Old Testament texts. But that only puts us one step further back, because that raises the question of the economic system within which the prophets found themselves.

The number of positions held on Luke's economic perspective shows that this is not a moot question. He has been taken to be "evangelist for the poor,"[1] as well as comforter for the rich.[2] It has been discussed whether the community life described in Acts 2:44–46 and 4:32–35 represents a form of "communism."[3] In a recent work on wealth and poverty in Luke, W. Pilgrim[4] rejects that notion and says that these texts express an ethical concept that one should share according to need. Moreover, willingness to do so was a result of "their marvelous sense of Christian community." But he does not answer the question why this sense of "Christian

1. H. J. Degenhardt, *Lukas Evangelist der Armen* (Stuttgart, W. Ger.: Katholisches Bibelwerk, 1965).

2. A. Mayer, *Der Zensierte Jesus: Soziologie des Neuen Testaments* (Freiburg, W. Ger.: Walter, 1983).

3. K. Lake in F. J. Foakes Jackson and K. Lake, eds., *The Beginnings of Christianity* (London: Macmillan & Co., 1933), 5:140–49.

4. *Good News to the Poor: Wealth and Poverty in Luke-Acts* (Minneapolis: Augsburg Publishing House, 1981), 150.

community" found just this expression. What were the underlying conceptions and presuppositions when the result did not become communism in the meaning of "common ownership," but rather "sharing according to need"? Pilgrim mentions the Greek notion that "friends have everything in common" as a partial explanation. A more comprehensive look at the total economic system is needed, however.

In chapter 4 we looked at the social and economic system as it was determined by the elites. They defined the terms for the patron–client relationship and they had the power to control wealth and land. They also had at their disposal the "great tradition," teaching, rites, and symbols that supported their point of view. Underneath this superstructure, however, the traditions of the villages and the peasant population continued to govern their daily lives and dealings. But it is much more difficult to get information about these traditions. Literary documents as well as historical remains in art and architecture almost exclusively come from the upper classes. It is difficult to find evidence for the mode of thinking among peasants or the urban poor. Sometimes it exists in scattered fragments.[5] For attempts at a reconstruction, models from present-day anthropological studies or historical studies from a later period are of great help. I suggest that social anthropological studies of the concept of "limited good" and of "the moral economy of the peasant" will provide helpful models to understand Luke's pattern of thought. The value of these models must be judged in use. Do they illuminate the material at hand so that we are better able to understand underlying processes?

"THE LIMITED GOOD SOCIETY"

Within ancient economy, much of the basic structure of "economic" thinking was the same among rulers and ruled, but there was an enormous inequality in terms of the power held. A typical element in peasant economy thus is the limited amount of power available to control one's situation. Not only power, but all other resources were in limited supply. The anthropologist G. Foster has argued that the basis for thinking about goods and the distribution

5. See W. Donlan, *The Aristocratic Ideal in Ancient Greece* (Lawrence, Kans.: Coronado Press, 1980).

of goods in peasant societies is the idea of the "limited good."[6] Foster summarizes his thesis in this way:

> By "image of limited good" I mean that broad areas of peasant behavior are patterned in such fashion as to suggest that peasants view their social, economic, and natural universes—their total environment—as one in which all of the desired things in life such as land, wealth, health, friendship and love, manliness and honor, respect and status, power and influence, security and safety, *exist in finite quantity* and *are always in short supply,* as far as the peasant is concerned. . . . There is *no way directly within peasant power to increase the available quantities.*[7]

This situation frequently leads to a defensive strategy vis-à-vis other villagers. The main concern of villagers is to protect that which they have, since increase in goods for one person will always have to be at the expense of others. Foster found this model worked not only for material goods but for immaterial goods as well. The underlying premise for this model is that a peasant society is a closed system. Foster's model will explain how peasants view the natural and social resources of the village and the immediate area.

The model of "limited good" has been much discussed. One of the alternatives to it, suggested by J. R. Gregory, is called "expectation of circumstantially balanced reciprocity."[8] The model by Gregory is more modest in its scope in that it only applies to material goods. The main difference from the idea of "limited good" (by Gregory termed the "zero-sum-idea") is that Gregory's model does not imply that the quantity of goods is ultimately limited. Gregory based his theories on the study of the Mopan village in Mexico, where the villagers considered it perfectly possible that goods could increase in quantity. Actually, increase in wealth through the introduction from the outside of modern market exchange into the village economy was the characteristic element of change during the period in which Gregory studied the village. But the basic philosophy of the village was not totally

6. "Peasant Society and the Image of Limited Good," *American Anthropologist* 67 (1965): 293–315.

7. Ibid., 296.

8. "Expectation of Reciprocity," 73–84.

different from that of the "limited good society." Here, too, the basic idea was equity, the idea that all should share equally. The primary means of sharing enforced by expectations and social pressure from the village community was that of fiesta sponsorship by the rich men of the village.

Despite criticism raised against these models,[9] Foster's theory of limited good points to a characteristic aspect of an economy based on land. Since the main question is not so much the expansion of production as the allocation of limited resources, an economy based on land has traditionally resisted attempts at change. This holds true not only of the peasants, but also of the elite, of large landowners, and typically characterized the elite's strategy of expansion of landholding during the Roman Empire rather than experimentation with new methods. W. A. Meeks cautions that "the perceptions and attitudes about change which we take for granted in modern industrial societies are in almost every case inappropriate to the conditions of Greco-Roman society."[10]

Thus, these changes in the economy that were brought about did not come from the landholding class. There were "entrepreneurs" in Hellenistic society, in a period characterized by new settlement, colonization, and the creation of a new class of merchants and adventurers and traders. These changes may have increased the differences between cities and rural areas. There were, for instance, tensions between Galilean villages and Hellenistic cities.[11] It is worth asking if this element of conflict between a "trade economy" and an economy based on land comes into view in Luke's Gospel. This element, however, must not be overrated; it did not basically change the structure of the cities living off the land in the surrounding villages. The elements of change that were most noticeable may have been increasing pressure from the landowners and central authorities upon the peasants.

How did the villagers deal with the problem of unequal distribu-

9. See "Comments," in *Current Anthropology* 16:84–90, esp. by T. J. Maloney, who questions the way in which both Foster and Gregory presuppose a "mental set or cognitive map" as an explanation for the demand for equality. Maloney finds the "real present conditions" a more convincing factor.

10. *The First Urban Christians: The Social World of the Apostle Paul* (New Haven: Yale University Press, 1983), 19.

11. Freyne, *Galilee,* 101–54.

tion within a "limited good society"? Being without power to resist the control that the outside landowners exercised over them, their area of influence was limited to the village. M. Nash has summarized the way in which local control of the main resources in a peasant society is exercised:

> The chief capital goods in peasant and primitive socieities are *land and-men.* Land tenure is an expression of the social structure of a peasant and primitive society, and the allocation of land results from the operation of the system of kinship, inheritance and marriage, rather than through contracts and transactions between economic units.[12]

Consequently, capital or economic chance may not be permitted to work in such a way that they disrupt traditional values and norms of the society. In many such societies, there is, therefore, a leveling mechanism that assures that accumulated resources are used for social ends. These ends are not necessarily economic or productive; rather, they may be geared towards preventing accumulation of capital and growth of economic inequality. This leveling mechanism can take the form of large feasts: for instance, the fiestas in Mexico or the potlatches of the West Coast of North America.

The kind of leveling mechanism and the form of social pressure are indicators of the level of social organization of a particular society. For instance, the use of potlatches is typical of societies in which the central authority (state) is distant and has little power in the local community. Potlatches, put on by a chief, are a way of dealing with the problem of inequality within a community with weak leadership and with unclear structures of authority. They are a way to share private wealth with the community; at the same time, this wealth is transformed into social status for the giver of the potlatch. Thus, such sharing of wealth in order to gain status is a way to solve the problem of inequality within a society with high demands for solidarity, but with a weak and undefined leadership.

"THE MORAL ECONOMY OF THE PEASANT"

The idea of "the limited good society" was a perspective shared by peasants and landowning elite in the Greco-Roman world. The

12. "The Organization of Economic Life," 8.

main difference between the two groups was their positions at opposite ends of the power scale. Social pressure by peasants to share by means of feasts and other devices worked at the level of village societies with relatively small differences in wealth and power. But how do peasants perceive their situation in the face of enormous differences in power? How do they view the socioeconomic system at work in such situations? For an answer to these questions, we shall turn to studies of "the moral economy of the peasant."

The term "moral economy" is used in studies of economic values of particular groups, most often of underprivileged groups.[13] James C. Scott gives this definition of the moral economy of peasants: it is "their notion of economic justice and their working definitions of exploitation—their view of which claims on their product were tolerable and which intolerable."[14]

This is an economy and a value system that is not based on market and profit but on *subsistence*. For a peasant household the basic need is for a reliable sustenance. The pressing problem for a peasant is that most of the time he lives close to the subsistence margin. He is always subject to forces outside his range of control: changes of weather and claims from landlords, patrons, or the state. Consequently, it is when we realize that we must start from the peasant's need for a reliable sustenance that we can examine "his relationships to his neighbor, to elites and to the state in terms of whether they aid or hinder him in meeting that need."[15]

Scott studied peasant economies with special reference to the effect of outside forces, especially market economy, upon this traditional economy. He found that the moral economy of the peasant represented a system of resistance to the impersonal forces of the market economy that introduced changes in tax systems and land tenure. Peasants tend to be conservative and skeptical of changes, since their basic interest is to protect their subsistence. In the face of claims on the surplus production from outside forces,

13. See E. P. Thompson, "The Moral Economy of the English Crowd in the Eighteenth Century," *Past and Present* 50 (1971): 76–136.

14. *The Moral Economy of the Peasant: Rebellion and Subsistence in Southeast Asia* (New Haven: Yale University Press, 1976), 3.

15. Ibid., 5.

their emphasis on subsistence makes them ask, What is left? rather than, How much is taken? Consequently, the critical moment when exploitation becomes so unbearable that it may cause protest is not linked to a certain percentage of their product; it occurs, rather, when there is not enough left to secure the sustenance of the family.

Peasant economy clearly represents a point of view "from below," and because it is based on the need for sustenance it tends to be conservative. R. MacMullen describes the peasant population in the Roman world in a similar way: "The central characteristic of the village [is] their conservatism. They and their population hovered so barely above subsistence level that no one dared risk a change. Conservatism in its root sense, simply to hang on to what one had, was imposed by force of circumstances."[16]

What is subsistence level? Modern studies of poverty have studied the consumption of food based on a per capita–per diem intake of food. Studies of preindustrial Europe have shown that a large number of people were so poor that not even their needs for a minimum daily diet could be covered, not to speak of their needs for clothes and housing.[17] Thus, not even the barest physical needs were covered. There is in peasant economy, however, a broader definition of "subsistence." Scott gives this definition of "a minimum income":

> While a minimum income has solid physiological dimensions, we must not overlook its social and cultural implications. In order to be a fully functioning member of village society, a household needs a certain level of resources to discharge its necessary ceremonial and social obligations as well as to feed itself adequately and continue to cultivate. To fall below this level is not only to risk starvation, it is to suffer *a profound loss of standing* within the community and perhaps to fall into a permanent situation of dependence.[18]

Thus, "subsistence" also implies being a fully functioning member of society and being able to meet social obligations. This definition could also be applied to the ruling landowning class within peasant

16. *Roman Social Relations,* 27.

17. C. Lis and H. Soly, *Poverty and Capitalism in Pre-industrial Europe* (Brighton, Eng.: Harvester, 1982), esp. 179–88.

18. *Moral Economy,* 10.

or ancient societies. For them, a much smaller proportion was needed to cover their physiological needs; much more, however, to cover their social obligations.[19] The basic difference, therefore, is that of *power* and *status,* and the various demands that are put upon people in different circumstances. The important category here is that of membership in a society, and the group to which one belongs and from whose members one seeks recognition. If one is a peasant and belongs to a village, there are certain social obligations within this community, and a failure to meet them may result in a loss of status and honor. These norms provided a perspective for a villager to evaluate his own situation, as well as to judge the behavior of others, for instance, richer members of the community.

In his study of an Andalusian village, J. A. Pitt-Rivers has also studied the way in which villagers viewed wealth and money:

> The values relating to money may be summed up as follows. They are not those of Protestant capitalism. The possession of money here is in no way a sign of grace, or a basis for moral distinctions; it is morally neutral. But *the ways in which it is acquired or spent are subject to moral judgment.* If it is gained at the expense of others, it is ill-gotten. If it is guarded avariciously, if it is spent in self-indulgence, it is evil. If it is gained by intelligence or hard work, if it is spent in meeting moral obligations, then it is good. Money is something which enables a man to be what he wants. It gives him power, power to be either good or evil. It bestows prestige only if it is employed in a morally approved manner.[20]

As with taxes or fees, the question is not that of percentage or sums: How much can one possess and still be a moral person? Rather, the question of money and possessions is seen within the context of social interaction and social responsibilities: How is it acquired and how is it spent? These are the values from the "limited good society." People within a community are part of the same social and economic system with limited resources.

Scott and Pitt-Rivers point to questions that we may ask of Luke when we attempt to draw a picture of the "moral economy" that operates in the Gospel. These questions from the point of view of

19. Cf. the study of French aristocracy in the seventeenth to eighteenth centuries by Norbert Elias, *The Court Society,* 41–65, on the connection between social class, prestige, and expenditure, and especially on the residences of the aristocracy.

20. *People of the Sierra,* 62–63.

the moral economy of the peasant shall be addressed as we examine key Lukan texts.

VILLAGE ECONOMY IN LUKE'S GOSPEL

How did the villagers in Luke's Gospel make their living? It was through work on the land, whether as peasants owning their own land, as tenants, day laborers, or servants. The various occupations that Luke mentions tell us how people made a living: apparently, these were so well known that there was no need to go into any detail about them. Work is a natural part of human life, used as an illustration in many parables or narratives (17:7–10, 31, 35, etc.). But Luke goes into detail when this normal situation does not apply, when people were not able to produce enough for themselves or became unable to meet their obligations. We hear about debts that people were unable to pay, famines, and people who went hungry. These events are signs that the normal situation, the social balance, is upset.

But what upset the balance? How did it happen that some people went hungry, while others had more than they needed? In most instances Luke does not tell how people got their wealth; they are just introduced as "rich" (e.g., 16:1; 18:23). There are a few instances, however, that can give us a clue to the way Luke thinks. Like Pitt-Rivers's villagers from Andalusia, Luke seems to think that there were morally acceptable ways to acquire wealth, as well as morally disreputable ones.

The parable of the rich fool gives a perfectly natural and morally acceptable reason for his growing wealth: "The land of a rich man brought forth plentifully" (12:16). In an economy based on *land*, natural elements like good weather or a harvest not destroyed by natural disasters were important factors. A good harvest could mean the difference between make and break for a smallholder, and for a big landowner it increased his wealth as well as the difference between him and the peasant, as in the parable of the rich fool in Luke 12. Besides natural factors, like the condition of the soil (8:5–8), *work* was also needed for a garden or tree to bear fruit (13:6–9).

Almost on the fringes of the world that he describes, outside the village economy, Luke mentions *trade*. That was a high-risk enterprise, but it also had high earning potential. Luke does not introduce this as something disreputable; he narrates it merely as a matter of fact (19:12–27).

Now, for the morally disreputable ways. Luke describes the village as a community in which many people were in a liminal position and had lost what they needed for a decent life. What they had lost, others gained: when some people became debtors, others gained the upper hand as lenders. In some cases Luke explicitly says that the rich got rich by exploiting the poor: for instance, when the unlucky servant tells the nobleman that "I was afraid of you, because you are a severe man; you take up what you did not lay down, and reap what you did not sow" (19:21). As with the rich, so apparently it was with their agents and servants. The behavior of soldiers towards the village population is reflected in the advice from John the Baptist: "Rob no one by violence or false accusations, and be content with your wages" (3:14).

Tax collectors were another group of people who could gain wealth by dishonorable means. This was particularly true of the tax farmers who had bought the right to collect taxes. We hear of Zacchaeus, who was so rich that he could afford to give half of his property to the poor, but he had gained it by dubious means: "If I have defrauded anyone of anything, I restore it fourfold" (19:8). This apparently was no singular incident; tax collectors were looked upon with suspicion as a group. This accounts for the admonition by John the Baptist to them as a group: "Collect no more than is appointed you" (3:13).

Reading through Luke's Gospel and discovering what people possessed, we realize that this was a personal economy on a very modest scale. Apart from land, which was the basis for their income, the items most frequently mentioned are *houses, food,* and *clothes*. We shall look at the use of these items from the perspective of Scott's definition of "minimum income": "In order to be a fully functioning member of village society, a household needs a certain level of resources to discharge its necessary obligations as well as to feed itself adequately and continue to cultivate."[21] In Luke's Gospel we find a strong emphasis on the social

21. *Moral Economy,* 10.

aspects of the use of possessions, a use which served to integrate the user as a "fully functioning member of village society." Thus, we shall study how Luke describes the use of possessions by three major groups into which he divides village society:

1. Full members of the society. From these one expects a good, commonly accepted use of possessions.

2. Fringe people on the periphery of the village, or those who withdraw from it or who fall below the standards. Their deviance becomes visible in their use of possessions as well.

3. Rich outsiders, absentee landlords, or central, faraway powers. Their position is reflected both in their claim upon village possessions and in their own lifestyle.

Houses

There are not many references to houses in Luke's Gospel. It is taken for granted that everybody who was not an outsider or possessed by demons was living in a house (8:27; 9:58). Luke describes the construction of houses (5:19) and the process of building (6:48–49), as well as the cost of building (14:28–29). Moreover, some of the parables speak of houses, referring to activities connected with them: sweeping of floors (11:25; 15:8) or knocking at doors (12:36). Houses were lit and lamps were in common use (11:33).

The most important use of houses was to show *hospitality.* A large number of narratives and parables are set in houses, and they provide the room for the frequent dinner scenes in Luke; thus, they are connected with one of the most central elements of the social and economic exchange in the village community.

Luke gives little information about the size of houses. Since most of them were in villages, they probably were very modest. Luke does not describe any of the large estates with their houses or the city mansions in Jerusalem.[22] The temple in Jerusalem, however, is described as a splendid building (21:5–6), in terms of wonderment, quite similar to the way peasants in the Middle Ages were amazed at the sight of a cathedral.[23]

22. See N. Avigad, "How the Wealthy Lived in Herodian Jerusalem," *BARev* 2/4 (1976): 1, 23–35.

23. See, for instance, the description of Kristin's first visit to a cathedral in medieval Norway in S. Undset, *Kristin Lavransdatter: The Bridal Wreath* (New York: Alfred A. Knopf, 1958), chapter 2.

Food

Luke's villagers had a simple diet, mainly consisting of bread and fish.[24] Meat figures rarely: a calf is mentioned for a big celebration (15:23), or a lamb for the Passover meal (22:7). Other items mentioned are wine (1:15), figs (13:6–9), eggs (11:12), and grain (6:1). Even considering that "bread" *(artos)* in many instances may be used as a technical term for "food,"[25] this still is a very simple diet. It shows the basic characteristics of agricultural life combined with fishing, and this points towards Galilee and the area around the Sea of Gennesaret as its origin.

This simple, basic diet reflects a life that did not allow for much extravagance. But the villagers were not even guaranteed this simple diet. There is a strikingly high number of passages referring to famine or hunger in Luke's Gospel, in most instances with a contrast between some who go hungry and others who have plenty (1:53; 6:21, 25; 16:19–21; 15:17). These passages are part of Luke's pattern of contrast between the rich and the needy. Moreover, there are also a couple of passages referring to famine or hunger in the history of Israel (4:25; 6:3). Many of these references to people who go hungry occur within a typically Lukan reversal pattern of "from hunger to satisfaction," describing how God will turn around the situation and satisfy the hungry (6:1–5, 21–25; 9:10–17; 15:14–24; 16:19–26). For people who are hungry the basic need is to be filled and to have enough to eat. The word Luke uses is *chortazō* (6:21; 9:17; 16:21). There is no luxury implied in this word: it is used of feeding the multitudes (9:17) and of Lazarus, "who desired to be fed with what fell from the rich man's table" (16:21).

Luke emphasizes a trait common to the other Gospels as well, that food is a basic need for people and that they need it in a minimum quantity. This is presupposed in the Lord's Prayer: "Give us each day our daily bread" (11:4). The word that is here translated with "daily," *epiousios,* has been much discussed. One possible explanation is that given by T. W. Manson: "It appears that our

24. Bread is mentioned in 4:3; 7:33; 9:3, 13; 11:5; 13:20–21; 14:15; 15:17; 22:19; 24:30; fish, in 9:13; 11:11; 24:42.

25. J. F. Ross, "Bread," *IDB* 1 (1962): 461–64; "Food," *IDB* 1 (1962): 304–8.

Greek word may be the equivalent of the Latin *diaria,* the daily ration issued to slaves, soldiers, workmen, etc."[26] This word may also reflect the custom of making bread for one day's consumption (although this is disputed) or of keeping bread for the next day ready in the house (11:5–8). In the parable of the steward responsible for handing out food to the other servants, food is specified by the term *sitometrion*: "the ration, the measured allowance of food" (12:42). This term is also used of distribution of corn in Greek cities, for instance, as gifts from a benefactor. In distribution of corn and other gifts in Greco-Roman cities the system benefited the rich more than the needy poor.[27] Thus, when the gospel demanded "equal rations" and "a fair share for all" in distribution of food, that was a demand on the basis of the need of common villagers.

Food was not always a scarce item in Luke's world. In some instances, he speaks of a surplus of food. In evaluating the use of food in these instances, Luke uses a judgment that corresponds to the way in which Andalusian villagers judged the use of money. The possession of a surplus of food is in itself morally neutral, but the way in which it is spent is subject to moral judgment: "If it is guarded avariciously, if it is spent in self-indulgence, it is evil . . . if it is spent in meeting moral obligations, then it is good."[28] The morally good use of food is generally associated with good communal behavior among "full" members of the village; the morally evil use Luke frequently finds among the rich outsiders.

A surplus of food is primarily associated with meeting social obligations in the form of meals. Luke has a much larger number of meal scenes, in narrative sections as well as in parables, than have Mark and Matthew.[29] In Luke's Gospel a meal functions as an effective metaphor for the banquet in the kingdom of God. In other passages a meal may have another function. For instance, in 17:7–10 and 22:7 the interest focuses upon the difference in rank

26. *The Sayings of Jesus* (Cambridge: Cambridge University Press, 1948), 169.

27. A. R. Hands, *Charities and Social Aid in Greece and Rome* (London: Thames & Hudson, 1968), 96–97.

28. Pitt-Rivers, *People of the Sierra,* 62–63.

29. See 5:29–32; 7:36–50; 10:38–42; 15:1–2, 6, 9, 22–25; 16:19–25; 19:6–10; 22:14–22; 24:30–31; 24:41–43.

and status expressed at meals: a master sits at the table, while a servant waits on him. In most instances, however, and certainly when used as metaphors for the kingdom to come, Jesus' meals have the function not of creating distinctions, but of bridging them and including people. Meals are expressions of hospitality and giving, of gathering people from the outside into the smaller household circle. Thus, the main interest is upon who is invited to participate and for what purpose a host has gathered people together for a meal.

Luke 15 is an example of a morally good use of meals within the village community. In the two first parables (of the lost sheep and coin, 15:3–10) neighbors and friends are invited to rejoice *(synchairein)* together with the fortunate owner. A similar invitation to share the rejoicing is found in the celebration of the return of the prodigal son: "Bring the fattened calf and kill it, and let us eat and be merry *(euphrantōmen)*" (15:23). The found property and the son who had returned were recognized with a common celebration and a sharing of food. This celebration strengthened the communal links in the village by making neighbors and friends participants in the events. In the case of the prodigal son, it also served to reintroduce him into the community and return honor to his father, who had been dishonored by the behavior of the son. Thus, someone who had experienced good fortune and was in a position to feast was under obligation to share this celebration with other members of the village: this was the honorable thing to do.

The main moral issue is the way in which somebody who has been fortunate spends his or her fortune. Luke's value system becomes clear when we try to follow his use of the expression "eat and make merry" from 15:23 in various contexts. In 15:23 it was the honorable and good thing to do. This was not always so, of course, because it depended upon the circumstances.

Let us take the rich fool in the parable in 12:16–21. There was nothing morally wrong in the way he got his fortune; it was through a good harvest. He, too, wants to "eat, drink, be merry" (12:19). In his case, however, this is not a matter of sharing his wealth with others, of inviting other people in the village to celebrate with him and so to spend some of his gains on others. Instead, the invitation to "eat, drink, be merry" is directed solely at himself. He is an example of "wealth guarded avariciously"; he is concerned with building larger barns to be able to store his surplus. These would serve him as a guarantee against bad years, when the village smallholders might have to come to him and borrow grain at a high price. Thus, in the eyes of the common people of the village, the rich man's act was not only selfish at the moment, but was also an effective way to secure his position and thereby his opportunity to make other villagers more dependent upon him. This attitude of nonsharing, of laying up treasures "for himself," is judged as being identical with not being rich "toward God."

Finally, the rich man in 16:19 "feasted sumptuously *(euphrainomenos)* every day." The beggar Lazarus lies outside his gate while the rich man carries on his feast inside, probably with friends of his own status and group. The stereotypical expression of "rejoicing/feasting," together with the description of the rich man's luxurious clothes, puts this man into the category of the selfish, arrogant rich who do not share with others, who keep aloof from common and needy people. Thus, the description of the rich man clearly indicates a moral judgment; with his description of the exterior, Luke has indicated the character of this person.[30] If one followed the honor code of the rich in Greco-Roman society, the rich man was behaving in a perfectly normal and morally acceptable way, engaging in a "conspicuous consumption" befitting his status. Luke, however, has introduced a different perspective, that of the "moral economy of the peasant." He sees the social situation from below; the rich man is judged already from the outset of the story. He is a man who spends his fortune on himself and on people like himself, for instance, his brothers (16:27–31). He was a rich man who used his celebrations for social ends to strengthen his link with his equals.

Underlying the criticism of the "merrymaking" of the rich was the assumption that wealth acquired by rich was never shared with the common folk of the village, but circulated only among themselves. Thus, the inequality that existed in the first place was emphasized by the way in which the rich spent their wealth: not for

30. Cf. a similar literary technique applied by Henry James in describing Miss Chancellor's drawing room as an expression of her character, in *The Bostonians* (New York: Penguin Books, 1984), chapter 3.

the common good, but to protect their own position as a group over and against the needy people of the village. They withdrew from the village community, or had never been a part of it, and followed another set of norms. The best example of this is the story of Jesus at dinner in the house of a rich Pharisee (14:1–14), which will be studied in more detail in a later chapter. The parables of the "conspicuous consumption" of the rich are a good example of the point of view of the "moral economy of the peasant," and they also show the inequality in power between the rich and the peasants. A peasant could only make an appeal to God, the supreme power, that he would reverse the inequity.

Finally, it is also worth noting the villagers' criticism of nonconsumption of food as a form of withdrawal from the community. Popular opinion held that John the Baptist must have been possessed, since he did not eat and drink (7:33). Fasting could have many functions, but it always meant at least a temporary withdrawal from the communality of meals.[31]

To sum up, we can say that food had several important functions. First and foremost, it was necessary for the upkeep of life. Many references to hunger and famine describe the village community as one in which many people lived close to or below the level of subsistence. Luke, therefore, emphasizes that every person has the right to basic requirements of food. Food was also, however, an important part of social interaction in feasts and hospitality. The perspective from which Luke views this is clearly that of the common folk, the ordinary villagers. The main requirement was that food be used for common consumption, for the benefit of everybody in the village, especially the needy. Thus, severe criticism was directed against the rich who behaved in a way that set them apart as outsiders, following not the ethos of the village, but rather that of their own group, the (provincial) elite of Greco-Roman society.

Clothes

Clothes bear the same significance as food and are sometimes mentioned together with food: they belong to the basic necessities

31. See Bruce T. Malina, *Christian Origins and Cultural Anthropology* (Atlanta: John Knox Press, 1986), 200.

of life. At the same time they are bearers of social meaning, indications of status and of integration in community life (9:3; 16:19; 15:22–23). The description of clothing reveals the same picture of a simple life among most people. They wore a cloak *(himation)* as an outer garment (6:29) and under that a shirt, a tunic (*chitōn,* 3:11; 6:29). Poor people might have to go without a shirt; to be the owner of two tunics apparently was a sign that one was relatively well-off. In addition to this simple dress, people wore sandals (*hypodēmata,* 3:16; 10:4; 15:22; 22:35). Clothes were scarce among poor people, and thus objects for robbers (6:29), as with the man on a journey from Jerusalem to Jericho who was stripped of his clothes (10:30).

Clothes were part of the social pattern, a norm for everybody in the community. To go without clothes was not only a deprivation, but was also regarded as shameful. When one was unable to cover one's body properly, one was exposed to shame. To be without clothes, therefore, meant to be impure. Luke gives particular emphasis to this, going beyond Mark and Matthew, in his version of the story of the Gerasene demoniac. Luke introduces him as "a man from the city who had demons; for a long time he had *worn no clothes,* and he lived not in a house but among the tombs" (8:27). This verse serves as a bracket to the story of the expulsion of the demon, together with the concluding v. 35, which states that when the people from the town came out, they "found the man from whom the demons had gone, sitting at the feet of Jesus, *clothed* and in his right mind." To be naked marked exclusion from the village community; it implied a transition from human life into demonic existence. Likewise, putting on clothes marked the transition back into human society.[32] The dress code was part of the boundary mechanism of this society. A person who did not conform to minimum requirements belonged to the "outsiders." He was not part of the community, but was impure.

Probably the Jesus movement had an element of non-use of clothes as a protest, as a way to show withdrawal from community, in a way similar to fasting. For the itinerant missionaries to have no

32. Cf. the use of metaphors for "clothing" and "unclothing" connected with baptism and Christian identity in the early church; see R. Scroggs and K. I. Groff, "Baptism in Mark: Dying and Rising with Christ," *JBL* 92 (1973): 531–48.

sandals and only one tunic (9:3; 10:4), and to exchange no greetings on their way, signaled a withdrawal and independence from the larger society.

Within the village community, clothes as well as food served to make occasions special, to single out something from the ordinary. When the prodigal son returned he was given his father's best robe, a ring on his finger, and sandals on his feet; he was dressed for the great feast (15:22–23). These gifts of clothes were a great honor and signaled a new installation into his old rights, a reentry into his father's house.[33] It was a fitting mark for his transition from death into life in terms of his social life (15:24). Consequently, to mark this special occasion with extraordinary clothes was a symbol understood by everyone in the village.

It should be noted, however, that in Luke's narrative it is regarded as a totally different situation when expensive clothes were used not to celebrate a special event, but to claim a special status above ordinary people. The rich man who feasted sumptuously was also exquisitely dressed in "purple and fine linen"; moreover, this happened every day (16:19)! This description has the atmosphere of a tale from *The Thousand and One Nights:* the life of the rich is viewed from afar, from outside the gate of the mansion, and the difference in lifestyle is exaggerated. This man is described in the same way as the king's courtiers. "Those who are gorgeously appareled and live in luxury are in kings' courts" (7:25). In neither case, however, is the description filled with admiration. The wealth and power that is expressed by luxurious clothing is recognized, but viewed with strong criticism. In 7:25 the lifestyle of the mighty is compared unfavorably with the simple life of the prophet John the Baptist; in 16:19, luxurious clothing was just another indicator of the selfish life of the rich.

On a smaller scale, the robes of the scribes are signs of their social status and especially of their pretensions (20:46). Clothing as a bearer of symbolic meaning is a central part of the humiliation of Jesus before Herod. The "gorgeous apparel" that Herod and his soldiers put on him is a means of mockery; it serves as an

33. For ancient parallels, see R. Rummel, "Clothes Maketh the Man—An Insight from Ancient Ugarit," *BARev* 2/3 (1976): 6–8.

ironic contrast to his lack of power and status and heightens his humiliation.

LUKE AND "THE MORAL ECONOMY OF THE PEASANT"

In Luke's description of the community life of the village, we see a conflict over the control of the resources of the village. A traditional system of reciprocity, communal sharing, and village values is under pressure from the outside, particularly from the rich outsiders with much power and their own values. This is an integral part of Luke's literary style: he does not describe this as a conflict between systems or social groups. Rather, he describes it in the form of individuals typifying different actions and attitudes.

In this regard, there are basically three main groups of actors. First come the peasants, who are members of the village in the full sense. Second, there are outsiders to the village, who set themselves apart from the norms of community. They do not conform to the accepted rules for the use of food, clothes, or housing, and thus they threaten the purity of the community. The best way to picture this is to view the community as a circle with the common ethos and values forming a boundary. Third, there are the rich and the mighty, ranging from rich people actually living in the village to absentee landlords and the rulers at the center of power. They are outsiders too, viewed from the village, in that their wealth and their use of it set them apart. They do not follow the village ethos, but rather that of the city rich. Thus, they are "outsiders," but in this case it is not sufficient to speak of them as being outside the boundaries of the village. There is an enormous difference in power at work here, which makes the visual image of the pyramid more helpful: the rich are the power elite, who can exert downward pressure on those below them. Moreover, viewed from the perspective of the rich in the city, the city is the center, and the surrounding areas with their villages are at the periphery of civilized life.

In their use, non-use, or misuse of possessions (houses, food, and clothes), the various actors divide into the three groups. Consequently, the acquisition and the use of these items reflect the pattern of social interaction and the power structure at work in this society.

We have concentrated primarily upon the acquisition of goods and their use within the context of social interaction, and we have noted the downward pressure by the rich upon the peasants. Another aspect of this relationship between the rich elite and the peasant population is the restriction put upon acquisitions and use of possessions. Luke describes a society characterized by scarcity; in that sense it was a "limited good society." And there is no free access to these scarce means. The access is controlled through the power structure of the society, made visible in the system of unequal exchange in the patron–client relationship.

The power to give access to scarce resources was in the hands of patrons. Lazarus, for instance, did not have access to food, which the rich man could have given him (16:20–25). Luke indicates this unequal relationship between people and the control over scarce means by using the term "give" *(didōmi)* to indicate social interaction and exchange. Persons who have the means and the opportunity to "give" are in a position to be patrons to others. Here patronage must be understood in its widest sense, including also relations between relatives (father–son) and neighbors. When the prodigal son had spent all his money in a foreign land and found himself in want, nobody "gave" him anything (15:16). A neighbor who has bread, a father who has food, a man with resources like food and clothes, should give to his neighbor, his son, and so forth (3:12; 6:29–30; 11:8, 9, 11, 13).

Luke's Gospel represents a protest against the abuse of the needy by the rich. But what was his basis for his defense of the rights of the poor and the needy? This is not the place to go deeply into Luke's proclamation of God as the defender of the poor and the reverser of the might of the powerful. This aspect of the prophetic tradition of the Old Testament was a very strong impulse for Luke. So it is in no way to detract from the importance of that tradition to focus on the social aspect, Luke's patterns for human relationships and models for social interaction. What did Luke see as the foundation for the rights of the poor?

A clue to an answer is the way in which Luke speaks of the "needs" *(chreia)* that people have. A glance at some central texts will bear this out. In the exhortation not to worry about food, drink, and clothes (12:22–32), there is an interesting comment about people's needs. The first part of the exhortation says why the disciples of Christ should not worry about food and clothes, because "life is more than food, and the body more than clothing" (12:23). At the end of the passage, this general exhortation is repeated (12:29), and the reason is that the disciples shall "Seek his kingdom, and these things shall be yours as well" (12:31). There is, however, a comment inserted between the two halves of the argument. It first stresses the difference between believers and outsiders ("for all the nations of the world seek these things" [12:30a]). The second half of the verse recognizes the desire for food, clothes, and other necessities: "and your Father knows that you need *(chrēzete)* them." Here it is clearly said that all people need basic things for the sustenance of life. These needs are recognized also for the believers; they are not above them. But they can trust that God will provide for them.

The same recognition of the necessities of life is found in the parable of the man who got unexpected visitors late at night (11:8). This emphasis on the basic needs of people is most strongly developed in Acts 2:44–45 and 4:35. Most discussions of these passages have focused on the aspect of communal lifestyle and redistribution through the apostles,[34] but it should also be noted that the reason for this sharing was to alleviate the *needs* that people had:[35]

> And all who believed were together and had all things in common; and they sold their possessions and goods and distributed them to all, as any had need. (2:44–45)

Likewise in Acts 4:

> There was not a needy person among them, for as many as were possessors of lands or houses sold them, and brought the proceeds of what was sold and laid it at the apostles' feet; and distribution was made to each as any had need. (4:34–35)

The basis for the much discussed "communism" in Acts, there-

34. For a particularly helpful analysis of the meaning of possessions in these passages, see Luke T. Johnson, *Literary Function of Possessions,* 183–90, 200–203.

35. Luke sees this as a fulfillment of the legislation of the seventh year in Deut. 15:4–5 and thus a sign that the Christians were the true Israel; see Johnson, *Literary Function of Possessions,* 200.

fore, was *redistribution* to take care of people's *needs*. In this way the first Christian community was the fulfillment of the "peasant economy" that is underlying Luke's village ethos. For Luke, this was based on the teachings of Israel's Holy Scriptures, and he couched it in terms from Greek ideals of friendship: "Friends have all in common."[36] But we are here concerned with the common traits that can be summed up under the heading "moral economy of the peasant" and that characterize all the statements Luke makes on economy. The exhortation given by John the Baptist in 3:11 starts from the premise that all should have what they need: a tunic and food were the minimum for everybody. Although John addresses those who are well-to-do, insofar as they have more than the absolute minimum, he argues from the perspective of a person in need.

This perspective determines Luke's judgment of human relationships. Compare the statement by Scott, that we must start from the peasant's need for a reliable sustenance if we want to examine "his relationships to his neighbor, to elites and to the state in terms of whether they aid or hinder him in meeting that need."[37] This underlies Luke's criticism of the elites who do not share. Thc ideal figures are persons of high rank who are generous and thereby act as patrons, for instance, the creditor who forgives his debtor (7:41–42).

The pressure to share was especially strong concerning food. Meals and hospitality were the most important social obligations, and at the same time they functioned as leveling mechanisms, so that it is here that criticism of antisocial behavior is the strongest. Rich people who refuse to share are outsiders to the village community; they have their solidarity somewhere else.

It is within this context that we can make sense of Luke's argument in defense of an economy based on need, directed towards production for use, rather than upon an economy based on accumulation of wealth.[38] Luke, however, does not discuss economic theories; his form is that of narrative and history. He presents

36. Johnson, *Literary Function of Possessions,* 2–3, 187.

37. *Moral Economy,* 5.

38. Similarly, in "primitive economics," see Sahlins, *Stone Age Economics,* 215–19.

alternatives not in the form of models, but in descriptions of people and their behavior. To his modern readers, however, models are useful to "decipher" Luke's pictures and images.

We have not, in this chapter, dealt explicitly with the theological aspects of Luke's arguments. Instead, we have tried to show that Luke's descriptions and his perspectives indeed do make sense within a model from peasant economics. But they are all couched in "God-language." Luke saw the universe as undivided under the rule of God. Since the flow of resources was structured according to the *power* in a society, Luke saw them as ultimately subject to the power of God, the creator and keeper of life. This accounts for his grounding of his arguments in Scripture, particularly in the traditions of the restitution of the good order of society in the Sabbath and the Jubilee years.[39]

Before we conclude this chapter, it is necessary to emphasize that the value system of the village was not solely based on the contrast between the rich outsiders and the peasants. We noted that there was also a third group, that of the outsiders or deviants at the village level. Status in the community was determined by a person's access to and use of food, clothes, and housing. The access to these necessities was often determined by the restricting power of wealthy outsiders, but the norm for use was very much a result of control by the village community. Within the village there was a "normal" use of these resources. If one did not follow the norm, one became an outsider; or, put in cultic categories, one became "unclean" or "possessed by demons."

Thus, there are some important boundary mechanisms at work here. They are linked especially to these vital areas of life that are concerned with food, housing, and clothing. In Luke's narrative, the use of these possessions reflects the identity of the person in relation to the social system of the village as a whole. There are accepted uses, controlled by village consensus; but there are also unaccepted uses that, because they are outside the social control of the village, put the user or non-user outside of the community. The rules concerning food, housing, and clothing mark boundaries in

39. See particularly 4:16–18. Cf. Sharon H. Ringe, *Jesus, Liberation, and the Biblical Jubilee* (Philadelphia: Fortress Press, 1985).

this community. These boundaries were linked to values like purity and honor, and they were part of a network that was shared by both the rich and the poor. This is an example of a system of *common values within a patron–client relationship,* which S. N. Eisenstadt and L. Roniger mention as a common phenomenon in such relations.[40] Thus, a system of pressure and exploitation by the rich was interwoven with a system of common norms and values in some important areas of social life. This network of commonly held values served to strengthen the bond between patron and clients. To break with these values meant a drastic break with village community in its totality.

Here we have spoken in very general terms of village norms for use of food, clothes, and housing, and of values like purity and honor. In Luke's Gospel these "village norms" certainly were very specific laws from the Holy Scriptures, or derived from interpretation of these Scriptures. Moreover, the authorities of interpretation of Scriptures and thereby the upholders of these rules were the Pharisees, who were very much concerned with purity. Therefore, given the general pattern of economic exchange and Luke's perspective from "peasant economics" that we have laid out, it is now time to focus more specifically on the role of the Pharisees. Where do they fit in this pattern of social interrelation and economic exchange? We reached the conclusion that Luke's description of the village scene fits the model of the patron–client relationship: a very unequal exchange in forms of resources and power is combined with shared cultural and social (religious) values. This seems to be the accusation that Luke directs towards the Pharisees: that they held this ambiguous position within the socioeconomic relations between patrons and clients in Palestine.

40. "Patron–Client Relations," 71–72.

CHAPTER 6

Rules of Purity and Social Order: The Role of the Pharisees

Luke portrays the Pharisees both as people concerned with purity and as moneylovers concerned with social status. How can these elements be combined to form a meaningful picture?

Ancient economy was embedded in a total cultural and social universe, in which everything was connected. S. N. Eisenstadt and L. Roniger noticed that the structuring of resources and social relations in general exchange implies that there is given "some higher, transcendental meaning to these collectivities and to the social activities entailed."[1] For a systematic study, however, we need a model that can relate these diverse elements and point to the connections between them. Although coming from a different philosophical background and with a different set of interests than Eisenstadt and Roniger, the anthropologist Mary Douglas provides a helpful and suggestive model for the correlation between belief systems and social structures.[2] She uses body symbolism to relate social structures, cosmology, and symbols to an all-encompassing system.

1. *Patrons, Clients, and Friends,* 3.

2. Mary Douglas appears to be influenced by Durkheim and his structural-functionalist approach, and she also has a strong interest in groups and their boundary-making efforts. Both positions are criticized by S. N. Eisenstadt and L. Roniger in *Patrons, Clients, and Friends,* 19–27. The empirical background for Douglas's models is her fieldwork in East Africa. On this basis, she has developed a series of models of a general character, and she has written a number of comparative studies in anthropology, comparing highly different groups and cultures. Among her books, *Natural Symbols,* with a new introduction (New York: Pantheon, 1982), is particularly important as an attempt to establish a comprehensive model.

It is Douglas's main hypothesis that rules for control of the human body correspond to the social control exerted in a given society. Thus, there is a correlation between the restrictions put on the body of the individual, the self-image of a society, and its social structure and cosmology. Douglas sees a correspondence between attempts to preserve a social group's identity and purity vis-à-vis other groups, and restrictions on the physical body by way of purity laws to fight pollution.

In order to link social structure to a symbolic system, Douglas takes into account two key elements of social and cultural organization, which she terms "group" and "grid." It is not always clear what is implied by these terms, especially "grid," so I shall draw upon an interpretation of her work by S. R. Isenberg and D. E. Owen.[3] First, consider the explanation of "group":

> Group designates social pressure and is intended to indicate the extent to which an individual finds himself constrained and controlled by others. "Strong group" indicates a social situation in which the individual is tightly controlled by social pressure; "weak group" indicates the reverse.

It is at this point that the symbol system, the "grid," enters:

> There can be no pressure for conformity unless there is also something to which one can conform, no group identity without symbolic representation. The internal order of society and its shared understanding fall under Douglas' concept of grid. She describes grid as a system of shared classifications or symbols by which one brings order and intelligibility to one's experience.[4]

The weakness or strength of this system of classification depends upon its scope and coherence. A system that is full of contradictions or lacks coherence, or that has to compete with other classification systems, counts as "weak grid." On the other hand, "strong grid" is a classification system that is coherent, consistent, and broad in scope. Group and grid are not, however, independent variables; rather, they are linked together as dual aspects of a system of classification.

3. "Bodies, Natural and Contrived: The Work of Mary Douglas," *RelSRev* 3 (1977): 1–17.

4. Ibid., 6.

On this basis, Douglas outlines four main types of social organizations by using the combinations of group and grid, as well as the accompanying cosmologies.[5] The four types that result from this comparison are:

1. Weak group, but strong grid; that is, a strong system of shared values.
2. Weak group and weak grid. There is little social control and few shared values and symbols.
3. Strong group and strong grid, mutually reinforcing each other. There is strong social control as well as a system of common values.
4. Strong group but weak grid. Many members experience a conflict between the official system of values in their group and their own experiences.

LUKE'S PALESTINE: CONFLICT IN A STRONG GROUP SOCIETY

The social relations that Luke describes seem to fit the definition of a strong group. It is a group with

> high pressure to conform to social norms, a strong sense of group identity including clear distinctions between inside and outside and a clear set of boundaries separating the two, and a restricted set of condensed symbols expressing and reinforcing group identity.[6]

In Palestinian society as Luke describes it, there is a strong pressure from above. We have concentrated upon the economic pressure, but that was just one aspect of this unequal interaction. This economic pressure was based on power or threat of recourse to military force from the Roman governor, as well as from the Herodian tetrarchs and their soldiers (3:14, 19; 13:1, 31–34). Several of the parables about landlords and their stewards as a matter of course refer to the use of physical force in punishment (16:3; 19:27; 20:16). Luke is very much concerned with the question of power in social interaction in this community, as well as on a cosmological level. Confrontations between Jesus and Pharisees or

5. Aspects of cosmology or value systems compared in this classification are purity, ritual, magic, personal identity, body, trance, sin, cosmology proper, suffering, and misfortune.

6. Isenberg and Owen, "Douglas," 7.

other opponents frequently focus on the question of power (e.g., 4:31–37; 5:17–26). Frequent use of words for power, such as *exousia* and *dynamis,* point to a struggle for power as a central aspect of the history that Luke describes.

Wealth and superior status are used to exert pressure in the form of rent or payments of loans on those who are in a lower position. In the form of tribute to Rome and temple taxes, they are also a way to demand commitment and loyalty. But Luke's parables in particular point to a breakdown in loyalty to this system of power and control: tenants do not accept their duty to pay their landlord (20:9–16); a lord is accused of severity (19:21); patronage extended through hospitality may meet with rejection (14:16–24). While this commitment on the level of patron–client in a formal sense seems to be breaking down, it functions well on the level of the village community between people on a similar footing or in close relationships (e.g., 11:5–8, 11–13).

Another aspect of "strong group" was a strong sense of group identity combined with clear distinctions between "insiders" and "outsiders," with clear boundaries against outsiders. This corresponds with the norms against deviant use of possessions, as well as with the efforts by Pharisees and community leaders to enforce rules of purity. Purity laws, regulations for the observance of the Sabbath and for table fellowship, all served the same function of strengthening group identity and of separating members of the community from outsiders.

A third aspect of the strong group is related to this second one: it concerns the set of condensed symbols that expressed and reinforced group identity. Frequently, these were symbols and symbolic actions linked to the observance of purity laws, to the Sabbath, or to temple festivals.

From the point of view of Luke, however, this is a "low grid society," that is, a society in which many members experience a conflict between the official order and understanding of society and their own values and experiences.[7] Our study of the "moral econ-

7. This corresponds to a classification, using Douglas's model, of the social setting of most New Testament writings (except for John's Gospel), as well as of various Palestinian factions at the time (Pharisees, Zealots, etc.), by Bruce J. Malina, *Christian Origins,* 37–44.

omy" of Luke showed that he does not view society from the point of view of the Pharisees, the Romans, or the Herodian rulers, but rather from the perspective of those who were exposed to their power. They experienced a mismatch between traditional values and their own experience. Traditional values of the villagers were based on sharing and solidarity, but instead the villagers experienced oppression from landlords and rulers. The criticism that they voiced was always personal. The social order itself could not easily be changed; therefore, criticism was raised in the form of accusations against individuals who exploited the system. The result was that the legitimacy of these rulers was questioned, an effect which Eisenstadt and Roniger find typical of the inherent imbalance in the patron–client relationship.[8]

Another aspect of this breaking down of the basic solidarity within the community becomes visible in Luke's description of the poor. In several instances he pointedly lists them together with the unclean (7:22; 14:13, 21; 16:20–21). This indicates that poverty was not so much an economic as a social category. It implied not only lack of resources but of social standing, and an inability to meet social requirements.[9] Peasants who were put below subsistence level might also be unable to comply with purity laws, and thus they were put in a position of shame and dishonor. In this case, purity laws were part of the pressure put on the poor, working in tandem with the strong downward economic pressure.

Conflicts over purity laws provide a good illustration of relations between the physical body and the social and cosmological bodies in Douglas's model of group and grid. The control of the physical body is closely related to the control of the social body of a group, for instance, in the form of boundaries against outsiders. In a "strong group–weak grid" society there is great concern for purity both in the physical body and in the social body. Therefore, in a society of this kind, protection against pollution plays an important part to protect boundaries as well as internal structures and hierarchies.[10]

8. "Patron–Client Relations," 69–70.

9. Bruce J. Malina, *The New Testament World: Insights from Cultural Anthropology* (Atlanta: John Knox Press, 1981), 84–85.

10. Douglas, *Natural Symbols,* 107–24.

Luke describes the Pharisees and other leaders as intent upon upholding a strong group and strengthening the grid, that is, the correspondence between experiences and societal values. From the point of view of a ruling elite, a strong group and a strong grid situation is desirable, because that means stronger support for the ruling ideology of the group. In several encounters with Jesus, the Pharisees tried to influence their audience and to strengthen their commitment to purity laws. Purity laws were important because they were symbols of Jewish group identity. The Pharisees expressed their opposition to Jesus partly in an implicit way. They appealed to well-known norms that they regarded as self-evident for all Jews. Jesus' answers have a different character. They make his meaning explicitly clear and are a protest against the pressure by the Pharisees to strengthen group solidarity through purity laws.

A list of passages in Luke's Gospel dealing with the conflict will bear this out. Many of them have the Pharisees put in the role of opponents to Jesus, but it is clear that the concern for purity was not theirs alone. The passages concern purification of hands or vessels before meals (11:37–41), pure company at meals (5:29–32; 7:36–50; 15:1–2; 19:1–10) or otherwise (11:14–23), and rules for Sabbath observance (6:1–5, 6–11; 13:10–17). There is a consistent pattern in these stories. The criticism against Jesus does not give any explanation; it only points to popular assumptions like "it is not allowed" (6:2) or, equally self-explanatory, that a person is a sinner or a tax collector (5:30; 7:39; 15:2; 19:7). Thus, this was a criticism based on common knowledge, and leaders in the community invoked commitment to that knowledge. Luke presents this as a reaction that served to uphold the traditional pattern of society, and that gave legitimacy to oppressive structures.

In Luke's Gospel, Jesus is cast in the role of liberator from his first speech in Nazareth onwards (4:16–19).[11] In his answers to criticism from the Pharisees, Jesus takes as his starting point the need for a full human life. He sees healing as a way of restoring life by freeing the sick from the bonds of the devil (13:16), as "doing good" and giving life in contrast to doing evil (6:9). Moreover, it is

11. See Sharon H. Ringe, *Jesus, Liberation, and the Biblical Jubilee,* esp. 33–49.

the love of God that breaks the boundaries of the laws of purity (7:47; 15:7, 10, 24). Many of these texts deal with unequal distribution of resources—health, purity, honor—and the sinners and the ill were excluded from receiving their share. Jesus' answers function as a protest against this control of the distribution of resources, and point to values that would break the existing boundaries of Jewish society. Therefore, his protest against the rule of purity laws was a threat to the existing order of society. At the same time, Jesus showed with the power of his healings that he had authority from God to create a new order.

THE PHARISEES AND SOCIOECONOMIC CONTROL

This survey of some passages discussing purity confirms the traditional picture of the Pharisees as primarily concerned with purity. But this interest must be examined within its specific social setting, so that we realize the link between concern for physical purity and social order. The Pharisees were not only concerned with the boundaries of Israel. Through their attempts to control the physical body of people through purity laws, the Pharisees contributed to the preservation of the status quo of society. These stories focused on people who because of illness and sins suffered from uneven distribution of rights and resources, and who found themselves without access to the power of salvation. Thus, the question of purity was also a question of social control and the exercise of power.

What connection does Luke see between the Pharisees' insistence upon purity laws and their participation in socioeconomic exchange? We found that in ancient and peasant economies the flow of resources was controlled by power, particularly through some form of patron–client relationships.[12] "Power" is often used in a very wide and little defined sense. One definition of power is that it is "an ability to influence the behaviour of others and/or gain influence over the control of valued actions."[13] Another definition

12. See above, pp. 36–42.

13. R. Cohen, quoted by T. C. Lewellen, *Political Anthropology* (South Hadley, Mass.: Begin & Garvey, 1983), 93.

places power within the context of several related modes of social interaction: power, influence, commitment, and money.[14]

It is helpful to bear in mind these various interrelated forms of social interaction when we take a look at Isenberg's discussion of power in Greco-Roman Palestine. He works with a wide definition of "power" and starts from the presupposition that the meaning of power is culture-relative. It follows that

> for each society one must determine what its members consider to be the creative-ordering power or powers in their universe and also those powers which may disturb order. As power is mediated within a particular society it becomes particularized and definable. Each society may measure the access to power or possession of power in relation to an individual or a class or a social role.[15]

In the Jewish world the supreme power was God, and a person's sense of obligation towards family and society was bound up in an obligation to God. This obligation incurred indebtedness, which was discharged by means of redemptive media: in Palestine, that meant participation in cult and ritual, observance of law. The two main media of redemption and salvation were the temple and the Torah. They are *powers,* and access to them implies power. Thus, groups who thought that they were excluded from access to the redemptive media attempted to open that access. The Essenes tried to do that with their claim to be the true temple with the true cult; thus, they struck at the power of the temple in Jerusalem.

The Pharisees, on their part, claimed to have the authoritative interpretation of Torah, and thus control over salvation. Isenberg accepts the general tenet of Jacob Neusner's description of the Pharisees as a group primarily concerned with purity, but proceeds to argue the social significance of their interpretation of the Torah. He bases his argument primarily at Josephus's account of the Pharisees in the Hasmonean times, and suggests that the Pharisees were a "democratic" force challenging the authority of the wealthy aristocracy.

14. Talcott Parsons, *Politics and Social Structure* (New York: Free Press, 1969), esp. 353–472; see also Malina, *Christian Origins,* 77–87.

15. "Power through Temple and Torah in Greco-Roman Palestine," in *Christianity, Judaism, and Other Greco-Roman Cults,* Festschrift for M. Smith, ed. Jacob Neusner (Leiden, Neth.: E. J. Brill, 1975), 2:24–52.

> Pharisaic emphasis on the power of Torah interpretation threatened a significant re-ordering of the internal prestige system of the Palestinian Jew. At a time when the Temple priesthood and the Hasmonean dynasty held the political power of the society, that power was distributed according to the criteria of birth and wealth. Achievement expectations in the society would tend to be tightly programmed, with social mobility restricted. Indeed, given the probability that wealth would be inherited or associated with the Temple and political leadership, virtually all hung on birth. The Pharisees, by establishing a superordinate prestige system, challenged authority based on wealth and birth.[16]

Isenberg concludes by suggesting that the reason why the Pharisees could be perceived as a threat to the Hasmonean leadership was their support among the large mass of the population, as reported by Josephus.

Isenberg has correctly emphasized the power aspect (influence) of Torah interpretation and the authority implied in claims to have exclusive rights to interpret the Torah. He may also be correct in his evaluation of the historical situation, that the Pharisees were a "democratic" force attempting to end a system of access to power on the basis of birth and wealth. His reconstruction of the role of the Pharisees, however, primarily based on Josephus and rabbinical evidence, presents a picture with remarkable similarities as well as striking contrasts to Luke's picture of the Pharisees. The similarity lies in the way in which the various forms of social interaction (power, influence, commitment, and money) are related. Thus, the Pharisees' concern for purity was part of a competition for power.

In striking contrast to the picture that Isenberg draws, however, Luke does not portray the Pharisees as using their influence, based on Torah interpretation, *against* the power based on wealth and birth. On the contrary, he accuses them of joining forces with the power of wealth and privilege. There is a specifically Lukan dimension to the Pharisees in that at least some of them are described as participating in the exchange of socioeconomic goods, hospitality (7:36–50; 11:37; 14:1–14) and possessions (11:39–41). Furthermore, they are accused of being unduly concerned with money

16. "Power," 42.

(16:14). With this accusation that they were "lovers of money," Luke has identified them as belonging to a system of exploitation and economic pressure. And it is to a closer discussion of these accusations we now turn in a more thorough study of some passages that focus particularly on these issues.

CHAPTER 7

Purity and Almsgiving: A New Social Structure

Luke 11:37–44

We shall first examine two passages that have as their framework the Pharisees' concern for purity at meals and the observance of the Sabbath (11:37–44; 14:1–14). In both instances, there is a contrast between the concern for purity and the main theme of the passage: the Pharisees' involvement in the socioeconomic interaction in a negative way. As a contrast, Jesus sets up an alternative behavior. The forms of social interaction involved are *almsgiving* and *hospitality.* Thus, the meaning of "purity" is directly linked to social interaction. It is only Luke who has associated the Pharisees with almsgiving and hospitality. As forms of social interaction, hospitality and gift-giving are closely linked and show many of the same characteristics. It is, therefore, appropriate to hold Luke's advice about these two activities together.

Jesus' speech against the Pharisees and the scribes in 11:37–54 stands within the wider context of conflict passages in 11:14 to 12:12.[1] The form of this speech reveals its intended function: the accusations against Jesus' opponents are meant to undercut their authority as leaders, to take away their legitimacy as leaders in

1. The major themes in these passages are the power of God and the Holy Spirit. The terminology and metaphors used are best understood when seen in the context of the similes about lamps (11:33–36) and about light and darkness (12:2–3). The main metaphors are "eye and body," "light and darkness." Both passages have a revelation scheme: "Nothing is covered up that will not be revealed." (12:2; cf. 11:33). Thus, from the parallels in 11:33–36 and 12:2–4 we can expect that 11:37–41 will reveal something about the Pharisees.

Israel. To criticize leaders or members of an elite group of selfishness, hypocrisy, exploitation, and such is common in criticism "from below," from a position of little power. Criticism is divided between Pharisees (11:37–44) and scribes (11:45–54), and it is the first section dealing with the Pharisees that concerns us.

First, notice how Luke structures his pericope. In a typical fashion, he sets the controversy within the context of a meal.[2] Jesus' host, a Pharisee, criticized him for not washing before eating; that is, Jesus did not comply with the purity rules concerning meals. These rules were commonly known and therefore there was no need to explain them. The transition from the Lukan setting to the material from the Q source in 11:39–41 is not smooth. The Pharisee accused Jesus of not washing his hands, but instead of replying to this criticism, Jesus raises the issue of cleansing vessels before meals. The original form of the saying in 11:39–41 and Matt. 23:25–26 is uncertain.[3] Luke has:

> (39) Now you Pharisees cleanse the outside of the cup and of the dish, but inside you are full of extortion and wickedness. (40) You fools! Did not he who made the outside make the inside also? (41) But give for alms those things which are within; and behold, everything is clean for you.

Matthew has a somewhat different version:

> (25) Woe to you, scribes and Pharisees, hypocrites! for you cleanse the outside of the cup and of the plate, but inside they are full of extortion and rapacity. (26) You blind Pharisee! first cleanse the inside of the cup and of the plate, that the outside also may be clean.

It is possible that the original form of the saying ran something like: "You cleanse the outside of the cup and plate, but not the inside. Hypocrites: first cleanse the inside, and then the inside will

2. Luke's use of meal scenes has often been understood as his attempt to portray the relationship between Jesus and the Pharisees in more positive terms than Mark and Matthew do; cf. J. A. Ziesler, "Luke and the Pharisees," 146–57. But the present scene, as well as 13:26–27, shows that meals shared in this way did not necessarily result in a contrast between Jesus and the participants in the meal; cf. H. Moxnes, "Meals and the New Community in Luke," *SEÅ* 51–52 (1986–87): 160–63.

3. See the discussion in David E. Garland's *Matthew 23,* 141–50, and S. Westerholm's *Jesus and Scribal Authority,* ConBNT 10 (Lund, Swed.: C. W. K. Gleerup, 1978), 85–91.

be clean."[4] Jacob Neusner has argued that this saying would make sense within a Pharisaic discussion about purity rules. The position presupposed in this statement is that of the school of Shammai, which held that uncleanness from the outside of a vessel could spill over onto other parts of the vessel.[5] In the Gospels of Matthew and Luke alike, the parallelism between the outside and the inside of the vessel breaks down. The inner part of the vessel becomes a metaphor for "inner man."

Some scholars have accused Luke of misusing the original statement. David E. Garland contends that Luke may have totally misunderstood the original saying, and that he has a "modern" application of the statement, comparing the vessel to men's hearts.[6] Moreover, he finds that the reference to God's creation in 11:40 does not bear any relevance to the issue under discussion. Finally, he considers Luke so perplexed by the rabbinic discussion that in order to solve the dilemma, he took recourse to a popular theme, namely, almsgiving.

But is it likely that Luke just combined disparate elements without any coherence? Studied carefully within its context, Luke's version of the Q saying does not seem so strange. The first line of Luke's version is similar to that of Matthew: "Now you Pharisees cleanse the outside of the cup and of the dish" (11:39a). In the next line, however, Luke emphasizes more than Matthew that Jesus is not really concerned with vessels, but with people: "but inside *you are full of extortion and wickedness*" (11:39b). Luke does not speak in metaphors; in his version there can be no doubt that it is the Pharisees who are full of "plunder" *(harpagēs)* and "wickedness" *(ponēria)*.[7] The Pharisees are accused of desire to rob others of their property, to take by violent means something that belongs to others. The irony of this accusation against the Pharisees is not lost

4. Suggestion by W. A. Meeks related in Jacob Neusner, "First Cleanse the Inside! The Halakhic Background of a Controversy-Saying," *NTS* 22 (1976): 487.

5. Neusner, ibid.

6. Garland, *Matthew 23,* 144.

7. The word *harpagē* is common to Matthew and Luke. It is a word found in lists of vices, given the meaning of "robbery, plunder" (*Did.* 5.1; *Barn.* 20.1). Matthew refers to the stolen objects when he says that the cup and the dish are full of *harpagē.* When Luke says that the Pharisees are full of *harpagē,* the meaning is more that of greediness and rapacity, desire to plunder.

on the reader when seen together with the prayer of the stereotypical self-righteous Pharisee in the temple: "God, I thank thee that I am not like other men, extortioners *(harpages),* unjust, adulterers or even like this tax collector" (18:11).

The Pharisees are also accused of "wickedness" *(ponēria)*. In pointed contrast to their concern for cleansing vessels, they themselves are unclean and impure. Luke's use of *ponēria* links this passage to the mutual accusations of impurity and witchcraft between Jesus and his opponents and to the simile about the evil eye, an indication of envy and avarice, in the first part of the chapter (11:29, 34).[8] Consequently, the Pharisees stand indicted. Despite their concern for cleansing, they are reviled as unclean and impure. Purity was not guaranteed by observance of ritual purity; it was a matter of social relations and behavior toward others. Here Luke stands within a long tradition of opposition to the official cult within Israel, a tradition which emphasized the necessity of solidarity within the people and criticized the ruling class for its concern for cultic purity alone.[9]

To Luke, the real and grave impurity was that which consisted in plunder and greed. This was an uncleanness that was a result of negative social relations to others. Luke here goes one step further than he did in conflict passages about purity laws. There he presented purity laws as a support for an oppressive society; with their concern for purity, the Pharisees prevented people's needs from being met. Now the accusation is much more direct. Luke sees a direct link between their concern for purity laws and their exploitation of people. The very Pharisees who are most eager to be ritually pure and to make society clean through the observance of purity laws are themselves unclean because they are greedy, plunderous, and wicked. Consequently, their claim to leadership is illegitimate. In terms of M. Sahlins's classification system, this is "negative reciprocity," "the antisocial extreme"; it is taking from a client without giving anything in return. This is an accusation that frequently is voiced against leaders from common people.[10]

8. T. W. Manson, *Sayings of Jesus,* 93.

9. Jacob Neusner, *The Idea of Purity in Ancient Judaism,* SJLA 1 (Leiden, Neth.: E. J. Brill, 1973), 50–54.

10. Cf. W. Donlan, *Aristocratic Ideal in Ancient Greece,* 71–75.

ALMSGIVING AND SOCIAL RELATIONS

The exhortation from Jesus in Luke corresponds directly to this accusation. Matthew stays within the metaphor of clean/unclean, and therefore, speaks of "cleansing the inside." Luke's version, however, speaks directly about the Pharisees and their social relations: "But give for alms those things which are within; and behold, everything is clean for you" (11:41). This is a statement that speaks directly about giving alms: *ta enonta* should be understood in a concrete sense, "those things that are inside (i.e., the vessel)."[11]

But what is almsgiving? "Alms" appears here in Luke for the first time. Moreover, it is in a key position, a redactional reformulation of the Q saying. Luke 12:33 shows that this addition by Luke here is not accidental. In 12:33, he has a similar addition in the Q saying about not collecting treasures upon earth. In Luke's version it is introduced by the exhortation, "Sell what you have and give for alms." This is a parallel to other typically Lukan statements about selling and giving to the poor (6:30, 38; 18:22). Moreover, in Acts, almsgiving appears frequently, most prominently as a sign of the true worshiper of God in 10:2, 4, 31; compare 3:2, 3, 10; 9:36; 24:17. Thus, we have here come across a theme that apparently is very important to Luke. It is clearly linked to the central area of Luke's interest about money, the rich, and the poor, and thus it is a theme that has structural significance in Luke's Gospel.[12]

But what exactly does it mean? Why is almsgiving vital for purity? We can expect it to express the opposite attitude of "exhortation and wickedness" (11:39). But what does almsgiving mean in terms of the social relations between giver and recipient? This *social* aspect of almsgiving has not always been sufficiently considered. Frequently, the emphasis has been put upon the intention behind giving alms or the emotions of the giver. A recent study of charity in the Old Testament by H. D. Preuss is an example of this tendency.[13] "Almsgiving" belongs to a group of words classified

11. J. Fitzmyer, *Luke (X–XXIV),* 947; for another translation, "so far as what is inside [i.e., you]," see I. H. Marshall, *Gospel of Luke,* 495–96.

12. Consequently, it is not enough to say that almsgiving "was a favorite solution and a theme of Luke"; Garland, *Matthew 23,* 145.

13. "Barmherzigkeit," *TRE* 3 (1980): 215–24.

under the wider term "charity." According to Preuss, it is characteristic of the Old Testament that various words for charity connote not only an emotion or a feeling, but also a disposition that necessarily aims toward an act and that includes this manifestation. This observation is repeated so often that it almost becomes a litany.[14] The biblical passages under discussion, however, do not lend themselves to this contrast between "emotions" and "acts"; they speak without hesitation about acts of charity being performed. This contrast scheme established by Preuss reflects a culturally determined expectation that charity primarily has to do with our *intentions* vis-à-vis other people.

Another difficulty in interpreting "almsgiving" is caused by another modern notion, that almsgiving means giving trifling sums from one's abundance.[15] Almsgiving is seen as a strategy that is opposed to a real sharing of wealth, a way to keep the poor masses quiet and to avoid a redistribution of property. Thus, almsgiving becomes a condescending giving from the rich to the poor, in reality upholding the basic inequality of society. Both perspectives, that almsgiving and charity are expressions of good intentions and that they are merely trifling gifts from one's abundance, are widespread. Consequently, they are bound to color the interpreter's reading of Luke's Gospel. Against this background it becomes natural to speak of almsgiving merely as a "popular solution" with Luke, as well as to see Luke as a benevolent patrician.

Other perspectives are drawn not from present-day notions, but rather from attempts to see almsgiving in Luke's Gospel within a Jewish setting. K. Berger[16] emphasizes the function of almsgiving as expiation for sins, and also the demands for almsgiving as directed towards proselytes and converts to show solidarity with the group. The emphasis in an interpretation from this perspective is frequently upon almsgiving as a means to procure salvation. The main focus of our study, however, is to study the social relations

14. 218, 219, 222; also in discussions of the New Testament by E. Kamlah, 225, 227.

15. See the discussion in J. Nissen, *Poverty and Mission,* IIMO Research Pamphlet 10 (Leiden, Neth.: E. J. Brill, 1984), 82.

16. "Almosen für Israel," *NTS* 23 (1977): 180–204.

between people in Luke's Gospel, and it is in this light that we shall approach the question of the meaning of "almsgiving."

ALMSGIVING AND HOSPITALITY IN HOMER

We want to study charity and almsgiving as expressions of social relations. An example of such a study that can serve as a model for us is W. Donlan's investigation of the role of generosity and giving in social relations in the world of Homer.[17] It has frequently been argued that Greek society was very different from Jewish society, in that it did not attach any positive value to almsgiving to the poor.[18] Basis for the social interaction among the Greeks was the idea of *mutuality* between equals, not concern for the poor.

But this picture may not be complete, at least not for an early period.[19] The political organization in Homeric society is much simpler than in later Greek society. It is at a position of transition from a tribal structure to a more centralized chiefdom. This is the same organizational level that is found in many societies studied by social anthropologists: for instance, Sahlins's discussion of reciprocity as "primitive exchange" is based on tribal and chiefdom societies.[20]

There is an interesting similarity between the ideals of Homeric society as described by Donlan and the ideals in Luke's writing. Donlan finds that *generosity* plays a fundamental role as a structural feature in Homeric social relations.[21] Similar to Luke, he

17. "Reciprocities in Homer," *The Classical World* 75 (1982): 137–76; "The Politics of Generosity in Homer," *Helios* 9 (1982): 1–15; *Aristocratic Ideal in Ancient Greece*.

18. Most prominently, H. Bolkestein, "Almosen," *RAC* 1 (1950): 301–2; R. Heiligenthal, "Werke der Barmherzigkeit oder Almosen," *NovT* 25 (1983): 289–301. For a full discussion, see H. Bolkestein, *Wohltätigkeit und Armenpflege im vorchristlichen Altertum* (1939; reprint, Groningen, Neth.: Bouma's Boekhuis, 1967), esp. 68–180.

19. Bolkestein (*Wohltätigkeit,* 177) recognizes that there was an earlier strand of philosophy in Greece that speaks of God's special concern for the poor. According to Bolkestein, however, this tendency was never further developed.

20. *Stone Age Economics,* 206–9.

21. "The fundamental role of generosity as a *structural feature* in Homeric social relations is evident in one aspect of giving, which, at first glance, appears to be without political implication. Twice we are told by Homer that 'all strangers and beggars are from Zeus, and the giving *(dosis)* is small and kindly [*Od.* 6.207; 14.57]' " ("The Politics of Generosity in Homer," 5).

finds this generosity expressed through *hospitality* and *giving to the poor*. The central proof-text is a passage that says that "all strangers and beggars are from Zeus, and the giving is small and kindly."[22] Homer is distant from Luke in time, so I am not arguing that Luke is directly influenced by his writings. However, Donlan's discussion of Homer provides a model for a study of the function of almsgiving within a societal context, not merely as an interaction between individuals.

In the system of economic exchange, "generosity" belongs within the area of generalized reciprocity or "chiefly redistribution." Donlan's study is particularly helpful to us, since he, too, uses Sahlins's categories of generalized, balanced, and negative reciprocity. Negative reciprocity mostly occurs at the intertribal level. When negative reciprocity occurs *within* tribal groups, this signifies ruptures in the normally expected patterns of social relations.[23] Acts of negative reciprocity in relations between leaders and lesser leaders or between leaders and people are, for instance, killings with robbery and confiscation of goods. This behavior is regarded as normal between strangers and enemies, but it is totally unacceptable within the same group, the tribe. Therefore, "the existence of this sector of 'unsociable' economic transactions, as between strangers, suggests a deep undercurrent of political instability in Homeric society."[24]

One set of examples of balanced reciprocity is termed compactual, and it indicates strongly "the social aspect of economic relations. These are peace-making and friendship agreements, marital alliances, hospitality, gift-giving and gift exchange."[25] Hospitality and gift-giving to strangers are included here; on an intertribal level, this is the alternative to fighting. The goal of hospitality and gift-giving on an intertribal level is to prevent strife and to preserve the social order. That is the reason why negative reciprocity is disruptive. It has no social purpose.

This emphasis on balanced reciprocity reflects a "primitive" social organization according to tribes. This is the way to preserve

22. *Odyssey* 6.207; 14.57
23. "Reciprocities," 142–43.
24. Ibid., 143.
25. Ibid., 145.

a social order and to keep peace. The chiefdom form removes the necessities for such transactions by making external relations between tribes into internal relations within the chiefdom.

The primary social and economic function of a chief is that of redistribution. "Chiefly redistribution" is a form of generalized reciprocity.[26] Generosity is a mark of the leader in this society. The relation between generosity and leadership varies in different types of social organizations. In communities with established rank orders, this rank structure influences economic relations in terms of noblesse oblige: there is an expectation and pressure upon leaders to be generous. In other societies, rank and leadership are achieved, then generosity becomes a "starting mechanism" to achieve rank, and generosity influences the hierarchical structure of the community.

On this basis, Donlan finds that generosity has a fundamental role as a structural feature in Homeric society.

> Unstinging generosity in these circumstances is both visible proof of rank and wealth and a source of prestige. In a tribal society the man who can afford to be and who is generous demonstrates his right to be leader. That this generosity takes place at the peripheral sector (stranger, beggar) simply confirms the right more strongly; and the giver gains in "moral" stature by adherence to the divine prescription that all strangers and beggars are from Zeus.[27]

Within the chiefdom structure, giving to a beggar or showing hospitality to a stranger is an expression not of balanced reciprocity, but of pure giving. Beggars or strangers are nonpersons, do not belong in the community, and are not economically productive. Thus, by giving to them, the group treats them as members: "A stranger welcomed into this orbit becomes a kind of temporary member of the group."[28]

The best example of generosity as a requirement of leadership is the description of the suitors of Penelope (the presumed widow of Odysseus), compared to Odysseus.

> The *oikos* of Odysseus had a reputation for generosity and especially

26. M. Sahlins, *Stone Age Economics,* 205–10.
27. "Reciprocities," 156.
28. "Generosity," 6.

> to have been kind to strangers. . . . The suitors, on the other hand, were the soul of ungenerosity, shamefully mistreating the beggar, violating the ordinances of the gods, showing they could not—in tribal terms—be chief in Ithaca.[29]

Penelope's criticism of this behavior (*Odyssey* 18.215–25) "shows the importance of generosity to any claim of leadership and the moral opprobrium that attends failure in this regard."[30] Ungenerous leaders behave in a shameful and dishonorable way.

Thus, in the *Odyssey,* the motifs of beggars and strangers, generous chiefs and ungenerous suitors have a signal function:

> To a Dark Age audience, understanding fully the social implications of generous giving, it will have been quite obvious that merely by their treatment of beggars the suitors showed their unworthiness to replace Odysseus as chief. It should be equally clear to us that the poetic device which has Odysseus return home a beggar was also a sociological metaphor, fusing the economic, social, political, religious and moral dimensions of a primitive chiefdom in a single integrating symbol.[31]

Donlan concludes his analysis of the economic exchange by drawing lines to the political situation. He finds that the predominant mode of exchange is that of balanced reciprocity, while generalized reciprocity or redistribution is of minor importance. This probably reflects a situation in which Homeric society was organized in "imperfect" chiefdoms, in which the tribal model predominated.[32]

Hellenistic culture in the time of Luke reflects a different political and social situation. There was no ethics of charity and almsgiving towards the poor. At the basis of Hellenistic ethics was not concern for the poor, but love towards one's friends. This is reflected in the fact that the Greeks and Romans had no specific words for almsgiving or giving to the poor.[33]

29. Ibid., 9.
30. Ibid.
31. Ibid., 10.
32. "Reciprocities," 172–73.
33. Bolkestein, "Almosen," 301.

ALMSGIVING AND A NEW SOCIETY IN LUKE

In Luke's Gospel, almsgiving has structural importance and serves as a symbol for his vision of a new society. By focusing on Luke's view of almsgiving and hospitality, his ideals for society will come into focus, including his views of how this society ought to be organized. His picture of Palestinian society is that of a society that is becoming stratified and divided, a society in which traditional norms of solidarity no longer work. It is a society in which solidarity first and foremost consists of solidarity between members of the same group or the same "class." This ethos reflects Luke's Greek-Hellenistic world.[34]

Almsgiving is Luke's alternative. But what did that imply in terms of social relations and social organization? There is a strong element of Old Testament influence behind Luke's advocacy of almsgiving, an exhortation to return to the "good old days."[35] But what was Luke's idea of a social organization, and how was that reflected in his picture of Christian groups or the leadership of Jesus and his disciples?

Almsgiving, as any other type of exchange, can be analyzed by means of three interrelated aspects: social distance, types of reciprocity, and moral values.[36] How much distance was there between the addressees of Jesus' admonitions to give, and the poor and needy? The rich man, the *archōn,* in 18:18–23 chose his riches above giving to the poor; that is, he kept his possessions to himself and distanced himself from the poor. His attitude, preservation of individual wealth and nonsharing, indicated social distance from the poor. The rich man in the parable in 16:19–31 showed the same distance. The Pharisees in 11:39 not only practiced nonsharing, they even resorted to exhortation and pressure of people. This is the antisocial extreme. The exhortation in 11:41, as well as the parallel directed against the scribes in 20:47 ("devouring widows'

34. F. W. Horn, *Glaube and Handeln in der Theologie des Lukas* (Göttingen, W. Ger.: Vandenhoeck & Ruprecht, 1983), 227–28.

35. D. P. Seccombe emphasizes the role of Isa. 58:6–7 in his work *Possessions and the Poor in Luke-Acts,* SNTV 8:6 (Linz, W. Ger.: Fuchs, 1982), 182–86.

36. Sahlins, *Stone Age Economics,* 198–99.

houses"), indicates that their pressure is directed against the weakest groups in the community who are exploited and who become "poor." Their rights are not respected. They are treated not as full members of the community, but as outsiders. The poor in Luke's Gospel are listed among the sick and the impure; therefore, they are outside the system of social exchange.

There is a difference in rank and power between the potential giver (Pharisee) and the recipients (the poor). The Pharisees can use extortion to take possessions from others (11:39) and they make claim to honor and respect above other people of the community (11:43). Thus, they hold power in the community, although in a negative way. Jesus' criticism in Luke 11:37–44 shows that they practiced negative reciprocity. Judged by the moral norms of the village, this was unacceptable. It was a violation of the community fellowship.

To give to the poor would mean redistribution, giving back that which they had taken. In terms of social interaction, it meant establishing a positive relationship. The Pharisees had to recognize the rights of the poor and accept some sort of link to them. In this way, they would act as responsible leaders, not exploiting people but rather giving to those in need. The moral value of this act is not explicitly expressed here. It is, however, part of the whole context of Luke's Gospel with its heavy emphasis upon God's option for the poor and his reversal of the present power structures to defend the poor. The possible result of the Pharisees' reversal of their attitude is clearly expressed: they would become pure (11:41).

It becomes obvious that Luke pictures the Pharisees as antitypes to good community behavior when we compare this passage to the story of Zacchaeus (19:1–10). Zacchaeus, too, had exerted pressure upon people *(esykophantēsa).* But he redistributed his goods by giving back *(apodidomi)* fourfold and by giving to the poor (*tois ptōchois didōmi,* 19:8). Here, too, the moral value of these acts is taken for granted. The result is clearly stated: "Today salvation has come to this house" (19:9). As a tax collector, Zacchaeus himself belonged to the outcasts, and his distribution to the poor means the creation of a social bond between groups of outsiders. The attribution of "salvation" to Zacchaeus, however, makes clear that through such acts former outsiders become insiders.

Jesus' criticism was directed against the social structure dominated by Pharisees, and he established an alternative structure based on almsgiving. Through their negative reciprocity, the Pharisees represented a break with the village solidarity. Jesus represents a return to the "old" values of internal solidarity. The exhortation to give alms to the poor without expecting a return was part of Jewish tradition, of wisdom tradition in particular (Prov. 14:31; 19:17).

In Luke's narrative, of course, we do not find a total transformation of the village communities to these "new" norms, which at the same time were very old. Rather, the exhortations to the would-be followers of Jesus (e.g., 6:30, 38; 12:33) show that these norms are put into effect by individuals who break away from the village community to form separate groups. So Luke's picture of Palestine is double. His description of a village scene at the time of Jesus forms the background for a layer that describes the "new" community. On the level of the narrative, Luke describes the conflict between Jesus and the Pharisees as a controversy over leadership of the same village community, and Luke proclaims Jesus the winner. This does not result in a takeover of the society by Jesus, however. Both Luke's Gospel and Acts reflect that the result was rather an exodus from that society to form new groups.

Consequently, the old solidarity norms of almsgiving became a sign of the followers of Jesus.[37] In this context, almsgiving takes on a new importance through its relationship to purity. An important function of purity norms was to draw boundaries between "insiders" and "outsiders." Jesus' protest against the purity laws of the Pharisees was also a protest against a structure of society upheld by these laws. The transformation of "purity," from a ritual concept to a concept of societal solidarity through almsgiving, meant a break with this structure and its boundaries.

This connection between purity expressed through almsgiving and boundary breaking becomes especially clear in the narrative in

37. See K. Berger, "Almosen für Israel," 180–204.

Acts 10—11 about the centurion Cornelius. He is a prototype of a believer; he was "a devout man *(eusebēs)* who feared God with all his household, gave alms *(eleēmosynas)* liberally to the people, and prayed constantly to God" (10:2). He showed the signs of a God-fearer: prayer and almsgiving. Luke relates these signs directly to the question of purity. Being a Gentile, he was unclean and therefore unfit for table fellowship with Jews. But his faith in God, expressed through prayer and almsgiving, had made him pure. This is the main point in the revelation to Peter in a dream about clean and unclean food: "What God has cleansed you must not call common *(koinou)*" (10:15). Therefore, Peter can say to Cornelius, "God has showed me that I should not call any man common or unclean" (10:28). And the link between purity, almsgiving, and prayer is repeated by Cornelius, when he relates the word from God that he received: "Your prayer has been heard and your alms have been remembered before God" (10:31).

In this narrative, Luke presupposes that the purity laws were used to uphold the boundaries of Israel. It shows Luke's link with Jewish tradition that he takes great concern to emphasize that it was through an act of God that the purity laws about table fellowship were redrawn. The demand for purity was not set aside. It was merely qualified in a new way. Purity was now understood as prayer and almsgiving; the latter could also be termed "righteousness *(dikaiosynē)*" (Acts 10:35; cf. Matt. 6:1). This new interpretation of "purity," breaking the borders of Israel open, was confirmed both by the outpouring of the Spirit and by the words of God.

In this way, observance of purity laws was made dependent upon social interaction. When Jesus says, "Give for alms the things which are inside, and behold, everything is clean for you" (11:41), the private and cultic is made public; the inside is turned inside out. Luke does not explain the "inside" of a person, sometimes spoken of as the "heart" (6:45; 12:34; 16:15), in psychological terms. Rather, it is explained in *social terms,* in terms of acts that show the relationships of a person with other people. The "inner" person actually is the human being in its social context, and the use of possessions in economic exchange and social interaction between people reveals the "inside" of a person or a group of persons. Luke's anthropology is based not upon psychology, living as he did in a prepsychological period, but upon observations of human interaction. And in contrast to Paul, who frequently focuses upon the person as a "sexual" being, Luke is primarily concerned with human beings as actors in social and economic interaction.

Thus, "almsgiving" or "giving to the poor" becomes a symbol of solidarity in the behavior of the community. In Luke 11:41, this demand is directed to the Pharisees as community leaders. They are accused of being exploiters, of antisocial behavior within the village exchange system. In his criticism of the Pharisees, Luke identifies with the village ideal.

LUKE 11:42–44:
CRITICISM OF BAD LEADERS

In the following verses also, the cultic and social practice of the Pharisees is confronted with their role in social interaction. The criticism of their tithing practice in 11:42 raises the same point: "But woe to you, Pharisees, for you tithe mint and rue and every herb, and neglect justice *(tēn krisin)* and the love of God *(tēn agapēn tou theou)*; these you ought to have done, without neglecting the other." Tithing is typical for the legal observance of the Pharisees in Luke's picture of them (see 18:12). Tithing of garden herbs went beyond that required by the law, and showed the zeal of the Pharisees.

The list of deeds that they should rather have done shows small but significant differences in the Gospels of Matthew and Luke. Matthew has "justice, mercy and faith *(krisin, eleos, pistis)*" (23:23), while Luke has "justice and love of God *(krisin, agapen tou theou)*." The variations point to major concerns for each writer. In Matthew, *eleos* reminds of his use of the quotation from Hosea 6:6, "I desire mercy and not sacrifice," in polemics against the Pharisees (9:13; 12:7). Luke does not use this quotation from Hosea, and has omitted *eleos* from his list. Instead, "love of God" has a similar function. In several instances, Pharisees (11:43; 16:13–14) and other opponents of Jesus (10:25–37) are accused of neglecting the love of God, a love which clearly also implies the love of one's neighbor.

The accusation that the Pharisees neglect *krisin* focuses specifically on their responsibility as judges of the people. "Judgment" is "the quality which fits one to be a judge, i.e., a keen sense of right and wrong, an inward rectitude, an unshakeable determination to uphold what is right and true and good."[38] The Pharisees are accused of obstructing justice, of not fulfilling their duties to be judges over Israel. This accusation against the Pharisees corresponds with Jesus' appointing the twelve apostles to be judges over Israel, to replace the old leadership (22:30).

Thus, the criticism of the tithing of the Pharisees also is a criticism of them as community leaders. But Jesus' conclusion—"these you ought to have done, without neglecting the others" (11:43)—limits the criticism. Once more Luke's criticism is directed not towards a system or the structure as such, but towards individuals misusing the system. Luke does not say that tithing was an unjust system that actually destroyed the social fabric. But he does say that the Pharisees, who practiced meticulous tithing, neglected their communal responsibilities expressed through "justice and love of God."

The accusation that follows in 11:43 once more emphasizes the close link between forms of economic exchange and social relations. It focuses upon the Pharisees' claim to *honor* and *status*: "Woe to you Pharisees! for you love the best seat in the synagogues and salutations in the market places." In 11:39–42, the Pharisees are accused of abusing their position to oppress people and to deal with them on the basis of negative reciprocity. The Pharisees had shown themselves to be bad leaders. Nevertheless, they had the audacity to claim the honors that went with leadership. Therefore, the "woe" discredits them as illegitimate leaders and confronts them with the final judgment.

This challenge to the authority of the leaders finds several parallels elsewhere in Luke. They are frequently clothed in the same form: Pharisees, and other persons presumably striving for leadership, make claim to honor, but this claim is rejected and they suffer humiliation. Those who are humble, however, will be rewarded by honor. The most famous expression is found twice in

38. Manson, *Sayings of Jesus,* 98.

Luke: "everyone who exalts himself [i.e., makes claim to honor] will be humbled, and he who humbles himself will be exalted" (14:11; 18:14). In both instances, "to exalt oneself" implies to place oneself *above others,* for instance, above the other guests at the dinner party or above the tax collector. People who make claims of honor compare themselves to other people and claim to be superior.[39] It also follows that they seek their recognition and honor from their own group, or from the public at large, by deceiving them of their true character.

In a typically Lukan fashion, the opponents of Jesus are accused that they want to show off as righteous "in the eyes of people" (10:29; 16:14; 18:9; 20:20). They make claims to leadership and honor, but falsely, since their claims are not combined with righteous behavior. Statements about the reversal of fortunes are part of the same context. The "woe" in 11:43 brings to mind the woes in 6:24–26; we expect a continuation, for instance, "you seek honor, but you will find shame."

In 11:44, Luke returns to purity language. The Pharisees are compared to unmarked and, therefore, invisible graves. When individuals walk across them unknowingly, they become unclean. There is an ironic twist to this conclusion of this series of accusations. The passage started out with the Pharisees' concern for purity, and ends with their being compared to impure graves. There is a series of accusations that is brought in to discredit the Pharisees and their claims: they claim to be pure, but they are impure; they are supposed to be generous, but they are exploiters; they uphold minute laws of tithing, but they are false and bad judges; they make claims to honor, but in reality, they are dishonorable.

Luke presents us with the traditional picture of Pharisees as a group concerned with purity laws and tithing, a highly respected group in the community. But he has added something that gives a new dimension. Luke's specific concern is their economic behavior. Economic exchange, either as extortion or as almsgiving, has a symbolic function. Economic exchange is regulated by social rela-

39. Cf. the use of *kauchēsis, kauchaomai* in Rom. 2:17, 23; 3:27; 4:2; see H. Räisänen, *Paul and the Law,* WUNT (Tübingen: J. C. B. Mohr [Paul Siebeck], 1983), 170–74.

tions, and these are expressed by differences in status and honor. Cultic and legal requirements are not dropped, but they are expressed through social relations and measured by social values. Thus, while the institutions of temple and tithing are respected and recognized, the Pharisees as community leaders in charge of upholding these institutions are discredited. In a fitting conclusion to this series of accusations, Luke 12 starts with an exhortation from Jesus to the crowds: "Beware of the leaven of the Pharisees, which is hypocrisy" (12:1).

CHAPTER 8

Hospitality and a New Community

Luke 14:1–14

In chapter 5 we noted that food and meals are important topics in Luke's Gospel. Food was necessary for life, and Luke stresses that every person has the right to nourishment. Furthermore, food consumed at meals is part of a social interaction. Finally, meals are metaphors for the kingdom of God. Luke sees the use of food from the point of view of "common people": it ought to benefit everybody in the community. Thus, the sharing of food in the form of hospitality becomes an important theme for Luke. In *New Testament Hospitality,* John Koenig offers a broad presentation of hospitality in Luke-Acts.[1] This theme is so important to Luke that it represents an excellent starting point for a study of Luke's view of the Christian community, in particular, of social relations and of missionary efforts.

We now turn to a passage in which Jesus contrasts the hospitality of the Pharisees with that which ought to be practiced by the community of believers. The term "hospitality" can indicate different types of social relations. Therefore, in order to bring to light the characteristic elements of the various types of hospitality, we shall study it as a form of reciprocal exchange of resources.

Hospitality is part of the social and economic interaction in a community, in the same way as gift-giving. S. N. Eisenstadt and L. Roniger say about the giving of gifts, "The latent purpose of gifts is to establish conditions of solidarity. . . . Generalized exchange, if

1. (Philadelphia: Fortress Press, 1985), 85–123.

successful, helps to establish the condition of basic trust and solidarity in society."[2] M. Sahlins says something similar about food and meals, but broadens the function beyond that of establishing relations: "Food dealings are a delicate barometer, a ritual statement, as it were, of social relations, and food is thus employed instrumentally as a starting, sustaining, or a destroying mechanism of sociability."[3]

Viewed against this background, Luke 14:1–14 reveals various patterns of social relations. The story is set within the context of a patron–client relationship. A Pharisee acts as host at a meal to which Jesus and a number of people from the village are invited.

From the title *archōn,* as well as from the list of guests (v. 12), it is obvious that this Pharisee is a prominent and rich man in the village. The setting of the story in 14:1–14 is similar to that of 11:37–54: Jesus is invited to a meal at the house of a Pharisee, and the Pharisees watch Jesus to see if he will keep the rules of purity or Sabbath observance (11:38; 14:1).

The narrative begins with Jesus' healing of a man suffering from dropsy on the Sabbath (14:1–6). Then follows Jesus' address to the guests and the host at the dinner (14:7–14), and finally, the parable of the invitation to the great party (14:15–24). In 11:37–44, Luke linked meals, purity, and almsgiving. In chapter 14, he combines meals, hospitality, Sabbath observance, and healing. Jesus defends his healing by pointing to human need; when somebody is in need, the rules for Sabbath observance may be suspended (14:3, 5). Twice the Pharisees are silenced and defeated (14:4, 6). Their strict observance of the law means that they confine the sick to a continued existence in a position of misery. By his healing, Jesus breaks the barrier set up around the Sabbath observance. Healing is giving to somebody in need. Thus, it is an event that is parallel to almsgiving and hospitality towards the poor.

Typically for Luke, he introduces the next passage dealing with the guests and the host at the meal with a character portrait of the guests: "Now he [Jesus] told a parable to those who were invited, when he marked how they chose the places of honor *(prōtoklisias)*"

2. "Patron–Client Relations," 52.
3. *Stone Age Economics,* 215.

(14:7). This is almost identical to the criticism of the Pharisees and the scribes (11:43; 20:46). Luke describes the situation as one of competition for honor, and therefore, one of conflict and comparison between people. The context is that of the behavior of guests at a meal, and it is to them that Jesus addresses his admonition (14:8–11).

A NEW GUEST LIST (LUKE 14:12–14)

The behavior of the guests is merely a reflection of the social dynamics of the meal. With the way this dinner party is set up, competition is inevitable. It is first necessary to take a look at Jesus' words to the host about the composition of his guest list. The focus of Luke 14:11–14 is the two guest lists with two alternatives of hospitality. The first list is the "negativc" guest list:

> When you give a dinner or a banquet,
> do not invite
> your friends or your brothers or your kinsmen or your rich neighbors,
> lest they also invite you in return, and you be repaid. (14:12)

Then follows the alternative, "new" list:

> But when you give a feast,
> invite
> the poor, the maimed, the lame, the blind,
> and you will be blessed, because they cannot repay you.
> You will be repaid at the resurrection of the just. (14:13–14)

The difference between these two alternatives of hospitality lies (1) in the social location of people to whom the invitation is extended, and (2) in their capacity to reciprocate. The result is two totally different modes of exchange: reciprocity between equals, and redistribution from the rich to the poor.

Luke is the only New Testament author to use the technical terminology of exchange based on reciprocity. He speaks of "repayment" *(antapodoma),* and of those who cannot repay *(antapodounai),* and of the generous host who will be repaid *(antapodothēsetai)*. What type of reciprocal exchange does Luke have in mind? How is it conditioned by the relationships between the persons involved?

In chapter 3, we discussed various forms of reciprocal exchange.

According to Sahlins,[4] they could be divided into three groups: generalized reciprocity, balanced reciprocity, and negative reciprocity. Generalized reciprocity is the most altruistic form, with less immediate and direct expectations of return. Negative reciprocity is the "antisocial extreme," "to get something for nothing." In 11:37–44, the Pharisees were accused of negative reciprocity through their rapacity, by exploiting people. Since this passage deals with hospitality, negative reciprocity is not an alternative.

Sahlins lists factors that influence the kinds of reciprocity that are used: "Kinship distance, while perhaps significant, is not necessarily decisive. Something may be said for rank, relative wealth and need, the type of goods whether food or durables, and still other factors."[5] He divides social space into the following sectors: house, lineage, village, tribal, and intertribal.[6] Forms of reciprocity used tend to move from generalized via balanced to negative reciprocity, as one moves away from the house-group towards the intertribal sector.

We now can study the guest list in Luke 14:12 in terms of kinship distance, rank, and wealth. At the dinner at the house of the Pharisee, kinship distance and wealth are decisive factors. The guests belong to a close circle of people. It ranges from the *house-group* ("brothers") to the *lineage sector* ("kinsmen") and the *village sector* ("friends" and "rich neighbors"). The guest list in 14:12 comprises the people closest to a person; compare a similar list in 21:16: "parents, brothers, kinsmen and friends." This is a very selective guest list, however, in that it does not include many people from the village sector.

The host himself is of high rank in the village. He is an *archōn*. His guests either are from the close kinship circle or, if they come from the village sector, are wealthy and associated with the host in friendship. Thus, this is a dinner for the "upper class" of the village. The function of hospitality within the group is "sustaining . . . mechanisms of sociability" among people on the same level. Through such hospitality, the group is sustained in its identity as a

4. Ibid., 185–276.
5. Ibid., 205.
6. Ibid., 199.

group; its group loyalties and its internal ties are strengthened. The end of v. 12 points out that this is done through reciprocity. This form of hospitality resulted in an invitation in return.

Normally, the obligation of a direct return for food sharing among near kinsfolk is very weak. It tends towards the pole of generalized reciprocity. There is an expectation of reciprocity, but it is usually not stipulated in time, quantity, or quality. Compared to this concept of hospitality and sharing of food in close groups, Luke's description of hospitality among the Pharisees is crude. By emphasizing the same status position and the expectation of a return, he portrays the Pharisees as individuals who use hospitality for self-serving purposes. He accuses them of keeping to themselves and excluding other people from their meals on social grounds.

This had two results. First, within the group itself, it created a situation of imbalance and competition (14:7–11). Second, it set this group apart from less fortunate members of the community and from outsiders. Their exchange mirrors their social relationship and strengthens their group cohesion and their dominant position in the village. Thus, there is a close correspondence between their socioeconomic exchange and their propagation of purity laws (14:1–6); both serve to strengthen their authority as leaders and the existing social order.

It is against this behavior by the wealthy that Jesus now directs his criticism. It should not be understood as a general prohibition of inviting relatives and friends. In the parables of the lost sheep and the lost coin (15:3–7, 8–10), the villagers who had found their lost property invited their "friends and neighbors" to celebrate with them. Similarly, when Cornelius expected Peter (Acts 10:24), he called together "his kinsmen and close friends." So there are legitimate reasons to invite kinsfolk and neighbors to celebrate. In the parables in Luke 15, the social setting is that of common villagers and generalized reciprocity within that group. In 14:12–14, on the other hand, Luke accuses the Pharisees and their social peers of selfishness for excluding less fortunate people from the village. Also, the explicit mention of expectations of reciprocity points to a more "economically" oriented system. It indicates a precarious social situation in which relations may be disrupted by inability to reciprocate. The instability of the situation is described in the scene of the competition among guests in 14:7, where everybody is fighting for the best seat.

In 14:13–14, the Pharisee is urged to extend his hospitality to new groups: "the poor, the maimed, the lame, the blind." These are people who were on the borders of or outside the village community. By Jewish law they were considered unclean. The Pharisee is asked to go beyond not only lines of kinship and close allies, but also the lines of purity so important for Pharisees. To invite needy and unclean persons meant to include them in a table fellowship originally reserved for people who followed the same rules of purity.[7]

Jesus does not here focus on the issue of purity, however. It is rather the socioeconomic aspect of the relationship that is stressed. He is concerned with the type of relationship that this invitation will establish between the Pharisee and his guests: "invite . . . because they do not have that with which to repay you" (14:14). Jesus urges a social system without reciprocity. How could that be, and what kind of system is this? This is called vertical generalized reciprocity, that is, giving from the top and downwards. In Sahlins's terms, it is chiefly redistribution.[8] Through this hospitality, the "poor, the maimed, the lame and the blind" are made members of the group, like the beggars at the house of Odysseus.[9] Compared to Homeric society, however, the characteristic element in this exhortation is that there is no expectation of reciprocity; not even gratitude or praise is mentioned.

The Pharisee is urged to extend hospitality in a continuous one-way flow. The in-group solidarity that could be expected within a close kinship group must be established with outsiders. And even more, it is a demand for a solidarity without an expectation of a return. Thus, 14:12–14 is a parallel to the admonition to give alms in 11:41. That also meant giving to those outside of the normal boundaries, without expecting a return. Luke presents a totally new social structure compared to that which the Pharisees repre-

7. See Jacob Neusner, "Two Pictures of the Pharisees: Philosophical Circle or Eating Club," *ATR* 64 (1982): 525–38.

8. *Stone Age Economics,* 208–9.

9. See above, p. 117.

sented. It is characterized by generosity and by redistribution. The flow of resources, of food, social recognition, and friendship, should not be kept within one group separate from the others; rather, outsiders were to be included.

In 6:32–36, Luke introduces a similar model within another example of the system of exchange. This time Jesus speaks of lending money: "And if you lend to those from whom you hope to receive *(labein)*, what credit is that to you? Even sinners lend to sinners, to receive *(apolabōsin)* as much again" (6:34). This form of exchange is clearly more economically oriented than hospitality. The fact that sinners are used as an example points toward a situation of exchange within a context of little societal trust. Therefore, social relations are dependent upon a quick return of borrowed goods or money,[10] that is, *balanced reciprocity.* Once more, the alternative is one of giving without expecting a return: "But lend, expecting nothing in return" (6:35). This is *redistribution,* a one-way flow from those who have to the have-nots.

Both in hospitality and in lending, the close group fellowship and solidarity that are implied in this exchange are extended beyond the usual limits. Furthermore, they are based on nonexpectation of a return, that is, on a continuous one-way flow of resources. These admonitions clearly are addressed to persons with resources who are in a position of leadership. The most characteristic element in the admonition is that not only are persons with resources urged to be generous, but they are also required not to expect a return of any kind. Compared to Hellenistic and later Christian texts, it is remarkable that there is no expectation of reciprocity, not even in the form of gratitude from the poor. The character of the social relationship is colored by this nonexpectation of reciprocity. This is the end of a patron–client relationship in a traditional sense.

In chapter 3, we discussed patron–client relationships and found that they are characterized by inequality, but also by exchange of different resources. A patron has social and economic resources; in return, a client can give expressions of solidarity and loyalty. Generosity from the patron can be translated into honor and

10. M. Sahlins, *Stone Age Economics,* 194–95.

power. Thus, the relationship becomes a paradoxical blend of asymmetry in power and mutual solidarity. What is the result in terms of social relations when a client is freed from any obligations of return? It means that the generosity on behalf of the patron cannot be transformed into power and prestige; it does not give him any advantages in his social relationship with the recipients of his generosity.

There is, however, a reciprocity involved. The host is promised a reward: "You will be repaid at the resurrection of the just" (14:14). So the basic concept of gift and returned gift is preserved, but the recompense is deferred until "the resurrection of the just." Moreover, it does not come from the recipient of the hospitality, but from God at the resurrection. God will pay back on behalf of the needy, the lame, and the blind. The idea is similar to that in the *Odyssey,* that "all beggars and strangers are from Zeus."[11] The expectation of a return, binding the client to an inferior position in the social relationship, is removed. Instead, the patron will have his reward from God, and thus, he becomes himself dependent upon God. God is the ultimate benefactor and patron; he will reward hospitality and almsgiving.

Luke presents us with a mode of behavior that is opposite to that of the Pharisees, who sought to be honored by men. Luke urges a sharing of resources without expectation of repayment, not even in the form of praise from men. Instead, he recommends a behavior based on never-ending redistribution. Those who are willing to accept the challenge to live a life on those terms are reassured that there is a reward. It is guaranteed by God himself (see 12:31).

REVERSAL OF STATUS (LUKE 14:7–11)

We now have established the pattern of social interaction involved at the dinner and are in a position to look at the exhortation to the guests in 14:7–11. How did this hospitality, with expectations of a balanced return, influence the behavior of the guests? The guests are kinfolk, friends, and associates of the Pharisee. Like their host, they used this occasion to seek to enhance their

11. *Odyssey* 6.207; 14.57.

status. They were engaged in a competition over rank: "they chose the places of honor" (14:7).

The "parable," or rather, the hortatory counsel,[12] about an invitation to a feast (14:8–11) is a combination of conventional sayings and well-known literary *topoi* that Luke found suitable here. Thus, they describe a typical rather than a specific social situation. The story illustrates Luke's picture of a society that functions within traditional norms of Jewish wisdom.[13] A guest is warned against choosing a seat of honor, lest a "more eminent man" than he may arrive, and he will be shamed in the presence of all the other guests when he has to give room. Instead, he ought to sit down in a secondary place, so that his host would call him "friend," that is, by an honorable name, and give him a seat higher up. This would give him honor in the eyes of all the other guests.

This story has all the ingredients of the honor–shame code of a village society.[14] Rank and status are based on comparison with others, and the norms used are well known within the village. If one acts outside of the norm by claiming a status that goes beyond one's recognized place, one is put down and incurs shame. On the other hand, if one acts with modesty and claims less rank than one is entitled to, it is only fair that one's rank be recognized and made visible to everybody present.

The guests in the house of the Pharisee are accused of breaking the fundamental rules of behavior in the community. Their competition for honor was a serious break with solidarity. Within Luke's scheme, this represents another example of the social situation created by the Pharisees. Their push towards balanced exchange in hospitality served to protect a group of villagers of primary rank from sharing with ordinary village people. But at the same time, this expectation of reciprocity created tensions within the group. Luke's picture fits well with the effects of a patron–client rela-

12. Fitzmyer, *Luke (XX–XXIV),* 1044.

13. This has led many scholars to harsh judgments of this kind of "morals." This honor–shame code is judged inferior compared to norms from their own social and cultural milieus; cf. J. Ernst, *Das Evangelium nach Lukas* (Regensburg, W. Ger.: Pustet, 1977), 437.

14. See Bruce J. Malina, *New Testament World,* 25–50.

tionship as described by Eisenstadt and Roniger: "All these factors tend to produce a certain pattern of interaction and struggle among members of the same social categories or classes, a pattern characterized by continuous contest, manipulation and perpetual imbalance."[15]

The general statement that is attached to this parable likewise falls within the moral code of the village. It expresses faith in ultimate justice: "For every one who exalts himself will be humbled, and he who humbles himself will be exalted" (14:11). The passive voice describes God's way of acting; it is he who humbles and who exalts. This statement is part of a series of reversal-sayings about God, starting with the Magnificat (1:51–53) and including the blessings and woes in 6:20–26. The second part of 14:11, "he who humbles himself will be exalted," corresponds to the promise to the host in v. 14: he who gives without seeking retribution from men will be rewarded by God.

CONCLUSION

The story in 14:1, 7–14 is an illustration of how economy is embedded in social relations in a peasant society. Social interactions in this passage include the Sabbath healing controversy, the competition for the best seats, as well as the "parable" with admonitions about behavior at a feast and the setting-up of a guest list. The social setting is that of the relationship between host and guests among a privileged group of people. Social interaction is characterized by seeking honor from other people, by extending hospitality with the expectation of an equal return, and by protecting the purity of Israel through a strict observance of Sabbath rules. In this way, the privileged position of prominent members of the town is preserved, while the sick, the poor, and the unclean are kept outside this system of exchange, and thereby excluded from the social relations as well.

Luke has Jesus direct strong criticism against this system of interaction: the Pharisees are silenced (14:3, 6); the honor-seeking guests are put to shame (14:9); those who exalt themselves are warned that they will be humbled (14:11). Luke introduces an

15. "Patron–Client Relations," 69–70.

alternative to this system of social interaction, an alternative based on "the moral economy of the peasant" and on concern for the village outsiders. The system of exchange represented by the Pharisees and their companions was a system of horizontal reciprocity. It was based on the interests of the leaders of the community, the rich host, and his well-to-do guests. Luke's alternative system was one of vertical redistribution. It was based on the needs of the outsiders and the lowly: the man with dropsy (14:2, 5); the guest at a lowly place at the table (14:10); the humble person (14:11); the poor and the impure who cannot reciprocate (14:13–14). In this new system of social relations, the one who humbles himself is awarded honor (14:11), the impure are healed, and the poor are invited to the feast and thereby included in the community.

Jesus' break with norms of purity and honor codes corresponds with his break with the system of exchange. It is a break with reciprocity within a restricted group, based on the ability to reciprocate. Instead, Luke introduces a system of redistribution in which the poor and their need form the starting point. Patrons are asked to relinquish their power, exerted through a system of reciprocities, and are asked instead to give freely in redistribution without expectations of return.

With this change in systems, Luke brings in God as the source of redistribution and as the great benefactor. Luke does not say something new about God, but he brings a common, accepted belief in God to bear on this particular situation. From Scripture, Pharisees knew well that God humbles those who exalt themselves. But Luke does say, "You are the man."

The redistribution that Luke argues in fact destroys the very basis of the patron–client system. This system was always a *person-to-person* relationship, although the element of mutuality was always mixed with inequality. A gift from the patron was followed by gratitude or some service on the part of the client. When a patron now is asked to forgo the expectation of any reciprocity, even gratitude, this bond between patron and client is loosened. There is no more binding the client in a social obligation of dependency. Thus, wealth cannot be transformed into power, rank, and status. This changes the whole attitude to power: there is no need to claim property or resources as one's own.

At one and the same time the giver stands in a client relationship to God. God is the ultimate patron and benefactor. One of the main characteristics of God's actions is that he practices redistribution through reversal (1:51–53; 6:20–26). Therefore, to give without expecting a return is to act like God, to be merciful, and to show compassion (cf. 6:32, 36; 7:42). And God, as the ultimate patron, will repay those who act like him. In this regard God upholds the system of rewards, but it is taken out of the social interaction between leaders and followers, patrons and clients. One's relation to possessions is indirectly one's relation to God. We now turn to a passage in Luke 16 in which this connection is made explicit.

CHAPTER 9

Lovers of Money—Slaves of Mammon: The Cosmological Implications of the Love of Money

We began our study of the Pharisees in Luke with a question: Why did Luke describe the Pharisees as "lovers of money"? This statement in 16:14, that the Pharisees were *philargyroi,* is in line with the descriptions in 11:37–44 and 14:1–14. But in what way does Luke here develop his argument? Does he give further reasons *why* it is wrong to love money, other than that it is a break with solidarity in the community? The accusation that the Pharisees were *philargyroi* is located in a passage (16:14–18) that is at the crossing point between the parable of the unjust steward and its interpretations (16:1–13) on the one hand, and the parable of the rich man and Lazarus (16:19–31) on the other. This central section in chapter 16 and the two parables throw light upon each other.

THE PARABLE OF THE UNJUST STEWARD (LUKE 16:1–9)

The parable of the unjust steward in 16:1–9 has been a puzzle for interpreters throughout centuries.[1] Many have thought it to be a major problem, that Jesus uses a dishonest person as an example. Therefore, much of the discussion has focused on the ending of the story. Did the original parable conclude with v. 7, the steward's instructions to the tenant debtors? Or did it include v. 8, the master's praise of the steward? Or were vv. 8–9 part of the

1. For a history of interpretation, see M. Kraemer, *Das Raetsel der Parabel vom ungerechten Verwalter Lk 16:1–13* (Zurich, 1972); and J. Fitzmyer, *Luke (XX–XXIV),* 1095–97.

original story as told by Jesus, but praise from Jesus and not from the master of the steward? Furthermore, what kind of economic transactions were involved? Did the steward act dishonestly when he reduced the debt of the tenants? In that case, he could be praised for his shrewdness, but not for his honesty. Or did he act legally, so that he could rightly receive his master's praise?

Some recent interpretations by J. Fitzmyer,[2] J. D. M. Derrett,[3] and K. E. Bailey[4] have attempted to situate the parable within a pattern of debts and business deals known from ancient and present Middle Eastern societies. "The rich man" of the story probably is an absentee landlord, a character well known from other Lukan stories. His steward *(oikonomos)* is his agent, who acts on behalf of his master (e.g., in renting out land, granting loans to tenants against the harvest, keeping records of these transactions, etc.).[5] Lending money was done at a commission, or interest, that was added to the principal. The bonds, however, frequently mentioned only one sum, which then included both the principal and the interest.

The most likely explanation of what actually happened when the steward reduced the debts is that he relinquished his own commission or interest on the loan. Interest could be exorbitantly high, so that twenty-five percent (16:7) or even one hundred percent (16:6) would not be impossible. The interpretations vary as to whether the steward actually gave away his own (unjust) commission, so that he truly deserved praise from his master for his righteous acts,[6] or whether he gave away his master's interest.[7]

From the perspective of patron–client relations and peasant economics, what can we say about the social dynamic and interaction in the story? There is a crisis in the relationship between the

2. *Luke (XX–XVIV),* 1095–1102.

3. "Fresh Light on St. Luke XVI: I. The Parable of the Unjust Steward," *NTS* 7 (1960–61): 198–219.

4. *Poet and Peasant,* 86–110.

5. Fitzmyer, *Luke (XX–XXIV),* 1097.

6. Ibid., 1098.

7. K. E. Bailey (*Poet and Peasant,* 94) holds that the steward made extras under the table, but that these were not reflected in the bond. Bailey argues that the steward gave away his master's profit, but that the master had to accept the deed in order to protect his own reputation as a generous man.

landowner and his manager, and the manager is accused of squandering his master's possessions. In this conflict, the steward protects himself by creating an alliance with his inferiors, his master's debtors, probably farmers in the village community. By doing them a favor by reducing their debts, he makes them his clients, who are indebted to him. In that way he can expect them to make returns, to receive him in their houses, and to give him support when he is deposed from his stewardship. This is an alliance that gives him leverage vis-à-vis his master. He protected himself by entering into reciprocal alliances with hopes of future returns.

Furthermore, the studies by Bailey, Fitzmyer, and Derrett in various ways point out that the background of the parable is an unjust system of exacting interest, taking usury on loans. Other passages in Luke likewise point to a situation in which farmers and smallholders were pressed down by debts (6:34; 7:40–42). This was an enormous pressure, and relief in the form of forgiveness of debts was an expression of totally unexpected grace. From the point of view of the debtors, this was an unjust system, creating a split between the rich and the poor. Thus, it is possible that the point of the story is that the steward did a right thing and behaved in a morally superior way by rectifying the injustice of usury. It served his own interest to create this alliance with the debtors, but at the same time it was in accordance with the "moral economy of the peasant."

This story has a change in perspective similar to that which takes place in many other passages: Who are the important people? To whom does one owe solidarity? In this story the steward shifted his solidarity, although for selfish reasons, from his rich master to a group of debtors. This was "prudent behavior" (16:8), and thus an example to "the children of light." The main point of comparison is provided by 16:4: "I know what I must do, to make sure that, when I have to leave, people will receive me *(dexōntai)* in their homes"; and 16:9: "So I say to you, use your worldly wealth to win friends for yourselves, so that when money is a thing of the past you will be received *(dexōntai)* into an eternal home."

The system of reciprocities will help us to understand this comparison. The steward acted wisely by entering into a relationship of reciprocity with his master's debtors: he gave them something that they needed, and was guaranteed a return in the future. The character of the reciprocity hovers between balanced reciprocity (business deals with specific and quick equal returns) and general reciprocity (close social relations with deferred expectations of return). But the main point is clear: the farmers will now become indebted to the steward, and will, therefore, be under a strong obligation to reciprocate.

The admonition in 16:9 to the "children of light" has a similar structure. The demand to enter into relationships, to "make friends for yourselves by means of unrighteous mammon," is followed by a promise of a reward: "so that when it fails they may receive you into the eternal habitations." It is not, however, these friends who reciprocate; *dexōntai* is here used as a passive and refers to an act of God.[8] The comparison is similar to that of Luke 6:32–36: even sinners lend and give with the expectation to get a return. The faithful, on the other hand, are exhorted to give and to lend without expecting a return. If they do this, they will have a big reward and will be called children of the highest. Similarly, the rich Pharisee in 14:7–14 is urged to stop his hospitality among equals, based on expectations of return, and instead to invite those who cannot reciprocate. Then he will be repaid *(antapodothēsetai)* at the resurrection of the just (14:14).

These parallels indicate that to use "the unrighteous mammon" to make friends is a metaphor for "giving alms," that is, to give to the needy.[9] Luke's use of the term "make friends" must be seen within his use of "friendship" as an institution in society.[10] Friendships differed from patron–client relations by being much more based on *equality* (cf. 14:10, 12; 15:6, 9, 29). It was a solidary, sharing relationship, and thus, totally different from the exploitation and inequality in power implied in a relationship between lender and debtor. To "make friends" by "unrighteous mammon,"

8. I. H. Marshall (*Gospel of Luke,* 621–22) lists three possibilities for the subject of the passive: (1) the angels, a circumlocution for the name of God; (2) the recipients of the alms; (3) the personified alms. From Lukan usage he finds (1) most plausible. Similarly, W. Grundmann, *Lukas,* 321.

9. Marshall (*Gospel of Luke,* 621) says that the persons who receive the alms become intercessors for the giver at the judgment; similarly, Grundmann, *Lukas,* 321. The angels as intercessors are another alternative.

10. See above, pp. 62, 70.

therefore, was the opposite of enslaving people in need. To "make friends" by giving to those in need had a liberating effect. It meant to put people on the same footing.

TWO MASTERS: GOD OR MAMMON? (LUKE 16:13)

In 16:10–12, Luke used the image of a steward who is responsible to his master for his dispositions of money and possessions. This image is in good continuation of the parable of the unrighteous steward and his relation to his master. Possessions, "unrighteous mammon," and "that which belongs to others" are there to be used wisely and responsibly. That is, the steward can be in control.

In 16:13, the picture changes to that of a servant and two masters. The servant has two possibilities; there are two masters whom he can serve, God and mammon. "Mammon" is no longer a resource that the faithful servant can control and put to good use. It has become another master who is able to enslave the servant. Thus, "mammon" is put over against God in a dualistic pattern. This wisdom saying comes from the Q tradition and has parallels in Matt. 6:24 and in the *Gospel of Thomas,* chapter 47. Linked to the context by the catchword "mammon," it has no original connection to the parable in 16:1–8;[11] but in Luke's redaction, it becomes of central importance in chapter 16.

The image of two masters is well known. In a Jewish milieu, it is found both in "psychological," ethical forms as well as in cosmological, apocalyptic forms.[12] The "psychological" form is found in rabbinic literature, which speaks of man as a slave simultaneously of his creator and of his "evil inclination" *(yeser)*.[13] The cosmological, apocalyptic form is found in Qumran literature. In Qumran, the praise of poverty and rejection of wealth was connected with the dualism of good and evil. According to this world view, there are two masters that compete: the Prince of Light is the

11. Fitzmyer, *Luke (XX–XXIV),* 1106.

12. S. Safrai and D. Flusser, "The Slave of Two Masters," *Immanuel* 6 (1976): 30–33.

13. Safrai and Flusser, "Two Masters," 30–31; cf. J. Marcus, "The Evil Inclination in the Epistle of James," *CBQ* 44 (1982): 606–21.

Archangel Michael, and the Angel of Darkness is Belial. These two masters exclude each other, and it is only possible to serve one of them. Thus, the Sons of Light abhor wealth, while the Sons of Darkness are connected with wealth (1QH 10:20–32).

Luke 16:13 has a closer resemblance to the apocalyptic dualism of Qumran than to the ethical dualism of the rabbis or of Greek and Hellenistic philosophers.[14] This is true also of Paul, when he speaks of being a slave either of God or of sin (Rom. 6:19–22). However, where Paul speaks of "sin" or "flesh" as the evil lord enslaving men, Luke speaks of "mammon." Although 16:13 is part of a common tradition, it fits well with a general tendency in Luke's Gospel. This points to differences in social milieus and in religious and philosophical traditions. Paul uses "flesh" *(sarx)* or "body" *(sōma)* as his central words to describe a person in his or her social relations, whereas in Luke's Gospel, "possessions" have a similar function. The use of "possessions" expresses social relations between persons and the play of power between them.[15] In the saying in 16:13, the power implied in possessions is personified. It has an almost demonic power; it is powerful enough to compete with God over lordship. Thus, a person can choose a master, but the emphasis in this saying is upon the situation of enslavement when this choice is made.

Why does Luke assume an absolutely adverse relationship between God and "mammon"? After all, many of the parables of the kingdom cast the master in a role dealing with possessions. Moreover, to enter into the kingdom or to be granted life in the presence of God is frequently spoken of in terms from economic exchange: as a *reward,* as a *repayment,* or as securing a *treasure* in heaven. So "mammon" cannot merely carry the connotation of "possessions" or "wealth." It is clearly very negative. Likewise, even when the addressees are urged to be wise stewards of mammon, it still remains "unrighteous mammon." What is the reason for this negative view of possessions?

Most answers within the context of historical scholarship have emphasized the Old Testament and Jewish background for Luke's

14. E.g., Plato *Republic* 888C; cf. Grundmann, *Lukas,* 322.
15. Luke T. Johnson, *Literary Function of Possessions,* 221.

views.[16] This explanation also needs to be put within the context of social systems. In chapter 5, we outlined some of the characteristics of a society in which all resources were held to be in limited supply. Here I will repeat some of our findings. It is commonly believed that it is not within peasant power to increase the available quantities of resources. Thus, increase in goods for one person always is at the expense of others. This creates a strong need to defend one's positions and a strong pressure to share any surplus. But in many instances, peasants stand in very unequal relationships in which they have very little power. This is a situation in which "a moral economy of the peasant" can be developed. It is based on the need for subsistence for the peasant's family. It is on these terms that rich members of a society are judged. J. A. Pitt-Rivers speaks of money as morally neutral in itself in his Andalusian village.[17] Money, of course, could be secured at the expense of others, and then it was regarded as ill-gotten. Although it might be gained through luck or labor, it became evil if it was avariciously hoarded or spent in self-indulgence.

In Luke, there seems to be an even stronger critical attitude towards possessions. "Mammon" is not morally neutral; within the context of chapter 16, it remains "unrighteous mammon." The parables in 16:1–8 and 16:19–31 combine various elements of wealth that is ill-gotten or spent in self-indulgence and conspicuous consumption. In the Lukan descriptions of the rich as negative examples, there is a clear implication that riches and "unrighteous mammon" are inseparable.[18] Luke's view of "mammon" must be seen in light of his view of riches and rich people.

Does Luke want to say that riches *always* are bad, that they either have come about as a result of oppression and exploitation or that they have to be used that way? In 16:9 and 16:11, mammon is stained by unrighteousness. This linkage between riches and unrighteousness can only be broken by faithful behavior, that is, almsgiving. As the term "unrighteous mammon" in 16:9 and 16:11

16. A good example of this approach is D. P. Seccombe's *Possessions and the Poor.*

17. *People of the Sierra,* 62–63.

18. J. D. M. Derrett observes: "It was matter of fact, as we infer from instances in the Gospel, that a man could hardly be rich in those days without neglecting the command 'love thy neighbour' " ("Fresh Light on St. Luke," 367).

indicates, "mammon" has the implication of a specific governing principle in the use and control of possessions and wealth. The channeling of resources and possessions is closely linked to power and social relations.

To understand what Luke means by "mammon," we may consider the examples Luke gives of wrong uses of possessions. The rule of "mammon" is expressed through negative reciprocity in exploitation (11:39), in hoarding (12:16–21), in conspicuous consumption (16:19–31), and in nonsharing with outsiders (14:12–14). In 16:13, all these examples of "unrighteous mammon" take on a new dimension, that of a cosmic power in direct opposition to God. When terms of economic exchange are used about God or about the kingdom, it is either in terms of benefaction and redistribution, or of reward for giving without expectation of return. Thus, the contrast that Luke 16:13 poses is one between two opposing forces, two totally different exchange systems and ways of structuring interpersonal relationships. Moreover, in apocalyptic fashion, the alternatives are posed as absolutes. There can be no middle way or middle ground for groups adhering to different masters.

LOVERS OF MONEY AND SEEKERS OF HONOR (LUKE 16:14–15)

His disciples are the immediate addressees for this alternative that Jesus sets up. They were introduced as the audience in v. 1. The audience from chapter 15, the Pharisees and scribes, have disappeared from sight, but are probably presupposed to be still present. And just when Luke has introduced the question of being under the lordship of God or mammon, the Pharisees reenter the picture as listeners and respondents (16:14). They respond by posing a challenge to Jesus; they scoff at him. "To scoff" *(ekmyktērizō)* is used only by Luke,[19] to express a reaction of scorn and disdain, of looking down upon somebody. Together with "to murmur" *(gongyzō, diagongyzō)*,[20] the word is mostly used to express the reaction of leaders of the people to Jesus. The reaction from the Pharisees thus is one of rejection and challenge to Jesus' teaching.

19. 16:14; 23:35.
20. 5:30; 15:2; 19:7.

The reason for the Pharisees' rejection of Jesus was their love of money. They were *philargyroi* (16:14). This is a redactional comment by Luke. It is like an "aside" in an old play; it gives the audience insight into the motives and the character of figures in the play. Lukes uses such "asides" quite frequently. It is particularly the attempt to pass as righteous and to be recognized and awarded honor in the community that Luke puts forth as blameworthy (10:29; 14:7; 18:9; 20:20). These asides are usually not observations of visible facts; rather, they give information about the hidden motivations and forces that make people behave the way they do. Whenever a new character turns up, the readers will always know if he belongs to the opponents of Jesus or not. These "asides" most often apply to the Jewish leadership and serve to discredit them from the outset of a story.

Consequently, the remark that the Pharisees were "lovers of money" stands within a Lukan pattern of discrediting remarks about Jewish leaders. The criticism follows the same pattern as in 11:37–44 and 14:7–14: the desire for economic gain went together with an unjustified claim for honor and recognition among other people (16:15). Thus, the very form of the accusation in 16:14–15 implies that it is part of Luke's narrative pattern. It is a literary motif that functions within the social world that Luke describes. It was with this observation that we started this study. To be "lovers of money" is part of a stock language of criticism of adversaries, particularly philosophical and religious teachers.[21] Now, after our study of the pattern of the socioeconomic relations between the Pharisees and "ordinary people," we realize that this accusation fits into that larger picture. Their "love of money" is part of a consistent pattern of social behavior that Luke attributes to the Pharisees.

In 16:15, Jesus answers the challenge from the Pharisees with a reversal statement, similar to other reversal statements in Luke's Gospel (1:51–53; 6:24–26). The verse divides into two parts: "You are those who justify yourselves before men, but God knows your hearts / for what is exalted among men is an abomination *(bdelygma)* in the sight of God." To pretend to be righteous refers

21. See above, chapter 1.

to the outward appearance, "before men." This is contrasted with standing in the sight of God, who "knows the heart," that is, the center of an individual's life, intentions, and actions.[22] With the contrast in 16:15b between "esteemed among men" and "abomination in the sight of God," Luke introduces the categories of pure and impure that were used in 11:39–41: *bdelygma* means something that is unclean and abhorrent. In Jewish tradition, it was characteristic of idols.[23] Thus, we find here the same combination of terminology from various areas as in 11:37–44. The social and economic behavior of the Pharisees makes them unclean, despite all their concern for purity.

Within the context of chapter 16, the accusations in 16:14–15 represent the harshest criticism of the Pharisees so far in Luke's Gospel. They are accused of worshiping not God, but mammon. Their wealth has become an idol that holds a demonic rule over them. They are bound in slavery to an idol, and therefore, they are impure, so that they cannot come before the presence of God. The accusation is similar to John 8:41–47, when Jesus speaks of the Jews as sons not of God, but of the devil. In vain they claim to be sons of Abraham (8:31–40). Luke portrays the Pharisees as slaves of mammon, not of God. In the parable in 16:19–31, moreover, it becomes clear that the rich who know the law of Moses without following it cannot be sons of Abraham. Thus, there is here no hope for the Pharisees. In 11:37–44, they were exhorted to give alms as a means to become pure. In 14:12–14, they were urged to procure a reward in the resurrection of the just by generously inviting the outsiders to their dinners. But in 16:14–15, there is no exhortation to change behavior, no possibility for reversal.

THE PHARISEES AND THE LAW (LUKE 16:16–18)

The following verses seem to underline this final judgment. The meaning of Luke 16:16–18 in this context is uncertain; there are

22. This verse is a parallel to 11:39–41 with its distinction between the "outside," which the Pharisees cleansed, and their "inside," which was full of extortion and wickedness. In 11:39–41, God was the creator of both the inside and the outside and demanded purity. In 16:15, God is the judge of the heart.

23. E.g., Isa. 1:13; 1 Kings 11:6, 33; 2 Kings 23:12.

two separate statements, vv. 16–17 and 18. Particularly, 16:16–17 has been much discussed, since H. Conzelmann made it his starting point for a division of Luke's understanding of salvation history into three distinctive periods.[24] In the Lukan version of this saying of Jesus (cf. Matt. 11:12–15), it runs: "The law and the prophets were until John; since then the good news of the kingdom of God is preached and every one enters it violently. But it is easier for heaven and earth to pass away, than for one dot of the law to become void." The addressees for this saying are the Pharisees. It is not until 17:1 that the disciples are reintroduced as Jesus' audience. The Pharisees are lovers of money and proud, but now they are threatened by the pending judgment of God (16:14–15). This judgment comes in the form of the kingdom of God that is being proclaimed (16:16). The kingdom does not make the law obsolete; rather, the Pharisees are held accountable before the law, no part of which is abridged (16:17).

What is the meaning of the reference to John the Baptist, in the context of a speech addressed to the Pharisees? This reference brings to mind another passage wherein Luke links John to the Pharisees. Luke 7:29–30 contrasts the way in which ordinary people *(laos)* and tax collectors received John's message, while the Pharisees and lawyers rejected it. The Pharisees did not heed the new period in salvation history introduced by John. Luke's description of their attitude and behavior also contrasts strongly with John's admonitions to soldiers and tax collectors (3:10–14). Rather, they are accused of the same sins of greed and exploitation.

The parable about the rich man and Lazarus in 16:19–31 strengthens this link to the admonitions by John the Baptist in 3:7–14. The rich man who finds himself in Hades calls repeatedly upon "Father Abraham" to help himself and his brothers (16:24, 27, 31). This is just as futile as John the Baptist said it would be to those who would not repent and bear the fruit of repentance: "Do not begin to say that we have Abraham as our father" (3:8). John urged his audience to bear the fruit of repentance before it was too late. To the rich man and his brothers it turned out to be too late, since they refused to act upon their knowledge of Moses and the

24. *Theology of St. Luke.*

prophets. When this parable is addressed to the Pharisees, it implies that Luke holds them to be in the same situation as the rich man: they were rich, they knew the law, but they did not act upon it in such a way that they were prepared for the coming of the kingdom. The rich man with his extravagant splendor and conspicuous consumption refuses to share with the poor Lazarus. He is an example of how possessions, in the demonic form of "mammon," take hold of people and put them into slavery. Thus, mammon is the single greatest threat to the observance of the law.

Finally, what role does 16:18 play in this context: "Every one who divorces his wife and marries another commits adultery, and he who marries a woman divorced from her husband commits adultery"? There is here the same hardening of the law of divorce compared to Pharisaic practice as in Matt. 5:31–32; in fact, even more so, since not even divorce on the grounds of adultery is allowed. Moreover, the full emphasis is upon the husband. This verse is introduced rather abruptly, and there are various suggestions why Luke has placed it here.[25]

There may be a simple solution to the problem of the connections between these seemingly disparate statements in 16:14–18. Maybe the combination of sayings is Luke's example of a series of vices: avarice (16:14), pride (16:15), licentiousness (16:18), all of which are signs of lawlessness (16:16–17). An indication of this, and also of a possible reason for linking this list to the Pharisees, is the parallel found in the Pharisee's prayer of self-righteousness in 18:11: "God, I thank thee that I am not like other men, extortioners [cf. 11:39], unjust [cf. 16:15], adulterers [cf. 16:18], or even like this tax collector." This may be a form of Lukan irony, to turn the Pharisee's prayer against himself. Similar lists of vices and virtues are frequent in New Testament letters. Thus, this is another indication that Luke has described the Pharisees as anti-types in 16:14–18.

25. One suggestion is that it is an example of the continuing validity of the law (Marshall, *Gospel of Luke,* 631). Grundmann (*Lukas,* 324) suggests that it is directed against the Pharisaic acceptance of divorce, which incidentally had economic consequences, related to the bridal money.

CONCLUSION: LUKE'S PORTRAIT OF THE PHARISEES

In his attempt to interpret the saying about the Pharisees in Luke 16:14, J. T. Sanders gave up and concluded that

> Luke's slander that they are *philargyroi* is without basis in the Gospel or the Acts. We learn from this brief statement, therefore, that Luke has a profound dislike for Pharisees and that he thinks of them as making light of Jesus, but the grounds for both escape us.[26]

The interpretation I offer shows otherwise. Interpreted in light of 11:37–44 and 14:7–14, Luke's statement about the Pharisees in 16:14 makes good sense. It is not a single, inexplicable utterance of dislike. Rather, it contributes to a coherent picture of the role and behavior of Pharisees within Palestinian society as described by Luke. Moreover, it fits well with the overall "economic program" of Luke's Gospel.

Luke measures the Pharisees against the "old" standards of the moral economy of the village. In Luke's Gospel, it is propagated by John the Baptist and present in the law. The coming of the kingdom in the proclamation of Jesus has made it even more imperative to follow the law with respect to economic exchange. This is exemplified in the story of the rich man and Lazarus as *redistribution,* giving to the poor, and in 11:41 and 14:14 as *almsgiving* and boundary-breaking *hospitality.* Luke does not present this as something "new"; rather, he phrases it as a return to the "old" ways with justice and rights for the poor and the needy. Thus, there is a connection between greed and nonobservance of the law.

In 11:37–44 and 14:7–14, the social relations between the Pharisees and common people were the focus for Luke's criticism. In chapter 16, this criticism is carried one step further. Luke puts the accusation that the Pharisees were "lovers of money" within a cosmological perspective of a world of two rulers and two principles. To love money was not just another sin, it was the ultimate sin of idolatry. In chapters 11 and 14, there was a possibility of repentance and turning away from evil ways. The Pharisees were ex-

26. "The Pharisees in Luke-Acts," 155–56.

horted to give alms and to show hospitality. In 16:14–15, there is no longer any possibility of repentance, no more than for the rich man in 16:19–31.

On a cosmological level, there is a total disqualification of the Pharisees. Luke takes away from them their right to God, to the law, and to the kingdom. On the cosmological level, "love of money" meant idolatry and slavery under mammon. On the human level, that corresponds to antisocial behavior. Thus, social and economic relations in Palestine at the time of Jesus are seen within the perspective of two opposing cosmic forces. The devil is an occasional force in Luke, prominent in the introduction to the Gospel and in its conclusion.[27] Throughout the Gospel, however, "mammon" is present as an opponent to God. It becomes visible in the opposition to Jesus.

The Pharisees in Luke's Gospel are not so much historical figures as *stereotypes*. His portrait of the Pharisees is designed to fit into the overall theme of his Gospel. This is similar to the other Synoptic Gospels. Their interest is not so much to give a historically correct picture of various groups as to lump them together as opponents of Jesus. Their main characteristic is that they are described as anti-types to Jesus and his disciples.

Thus, Luke uses his information about the Pharisees within his own narrative scheme. He is aware that they were concerned with laws of purity and that they believed in the resurrection of the dead. Luke includes these elements together with his own perspectives, and that makes for different emphases in his presentation in the Gospel and in Acts.

Luke uses much economic terminology and tells many of his stories from the perspective of socioeconomic exchange. Quite naturally, this influences his description of the Pharisees as well. Luke's portrait comes closer to Josephus's than Matthew's and Mark's in that it is put within a similar framework of social and political relations. In his *Antiquities,* Josephus portrays the Pharisees as good leaders and trustworthy politicians who were followed by the large masses in Palestine:

> The Pharisees simplify their standard of living, making no conces-

27. Cf. 4:2, 3, 6, 13; and 22:3, 31.

> sions to luxury. . . . Because of these views they are, as a matter of fact, extremely influential among the townsfolk, and all prayers and sacred rites of divine worship are performed according to their exposition. This is the greatest tribute that the inhabitants of the cities, by practicing the highest ideals both in their way of living and in their discourse, have paid to the excellence of the Pharisees.[28]

Josephus's portrait of the Pharisees, as examples of a simple life, opposed to luxury, and popular leaders of the masses, is directly opposite to that which Luke gives in his Gospel. But there is a structural similarity in their descriptions of Jewish society. Both work with contrasts between two groups of leaders. Josephus contrasts the Sadducees, rich and powerful leaders but without the support of the masses,[29] with the Pharisees, who lead simple lives and have the support of the people. In Luke's Gospel, the contrast is between the Pharisees and other leaders who exploit the people, and Jesus and his disciples, who act as benefactors. Thus, we find a literary pattern of stereotyped role models. This pattern probably was part of common descriptions of opponents, particularly bad leaders, known from both Jewish and Hellenistic literature.[30] It is understandable that Luke has attached this description to the Pharisees, since they were opponents to Jesus.

This does not mean that Luke's picture of the Pharisees is totally negative. In Acts, it is largely positive.[31] Even in the Gospel in several instances the Pharisees are described in a positive light. Some Pharisees warned Jesus that Herod wanted to kill him (13:33–34). Furthermore, it was some of the Pharisees who asked Jesus when the kingdom would come (17:20–21). Note, however, that these passages are not associated with the proclamation of new social and economic relations. It is when Luke focuses on the relations between the Pharisees and ordinary folk that his criticism becomes harsh. Thus, it is the larger context that determines his picture of the Pharisees.

28. *Antiquities* XVIII, 12, 15.

29. "There are but few men to whom this doctrine has been made known, but these are men of the highest standing. They accomplish practically nothing, however. For whenever they assume office, though they submit unwillingly and perforce, yet submit they do to the formulas of the Pharisees, since otherwise the masses would not tolerate them" (*Antiquities* XVIII, 17).

30. See above, pp. 6–8.

31. See below, pp. 159–60.

CHAPTER 10

The Economy of the Kingdom and Present-Day Challenges

Many studies have been done on Luke's attitude to possessions and to rich and poor. The starting point for this study was different, in that we tried to discern a pattern of social and economic interaction that makes the relationships which Luke describes intelligible. We found that pattern to be a system of reciprocal exchange of various types. Luke describes the situation in Israel at the time of Jesus as one of negative or balanced reciprocity. Rich leaders exploit and put pressure upon the peasants. Between themselves, the leaders are engaged in balanced reciprocity. Luke consistently directs his criticism at such leaders. In this study, we have concentrated upon Luke's criticism of the Pharisees.

LUKE'S ALTERNATIVE: AN ECONOMY OF THE KINGDOM

But what was Luke's alternative to the Pharisees and their antisocial behavior? A central point for Luke's proclamation of the kingdom is the presentation of Jesus as *benefactor,* based on his proclamation in 4:16–19, with strong overtones of the Jubilee year renewal.[1] A return to a situation of equality and justice for all, however, required a reversal of the present situation. Luke describes this reversal primarily in terms of socioeconomic relations within Jewish society, the relations between the rich and the needy, the powerful and the weak. Thus, Luke envisages a reversal

1. See Sharon H. Ringe, *Jesus, Liberation, and the Biblical Jubilee.*

that implied a central, forced *redistribution* of goods and possessions, prophetically forewarned in the Magnificat (1:51–53). This reversal was an act of God, and the divine redistribution was manifested through the acts and speeches of Jesus, the benefactor of humanity.[2]

This divine act served as the foundation for a new interaction among individuals and groups, likewise based on generalized reciprocity and redistribution. It was prophetically demanded by John the Baptist (3:10–14) and followed up by Jesus in words addressed both to his disciples and to his adversaries. In Jesus' proclamation of the kingdom, there are a large number of words for economic exchange. In several instances, Luke adds to his Q and Markan sources material that is characterized by terminology of exchange: negative, balanced, and generalized reciprocity or redistribution.[3] As a result, Luke's proclamation of the kingdom is colored by economic language. And it is possible to distinguish between different types of exchange, primarily within reciprocal exchange on the village level: negative, balanced, and generalized reciprocity, as well as redistribution on a local level.

When we are aware of this, it is easier to recognize patterns of social interaction, and to see Luke's alternatives more clearly. His criticism is directed against negative reciprocity in the form of exploitation of the poor by the powerful, as well as against a balanced or even generalized reciprocity among the well-to-do in which the needy are excluded. As an alternative, Luke argues for a system of generalized reciprocity and outright redistribution. It is presented from two different perspectives: in some passages from the point of view of the *giver,* in others from the point of view of the *recipient.*

People with resources are urged to be generous without limits. They are involved in a situation with great differences in power and resources, and they are asked to perform *redistribution.* The main characteristic, however, is the emphasis upon nonexpectance of repayment when they lend money or show hospitality (6:34–35; 14:12–14). The same structure is found in the exhortations to give

2. 6:20–26; 7:22; 9:1–6; 10:1–12.

3. See 6:34–36; 12:33; 14:12–14.

(didōmi). The nonreturn is not always explicitly mentioned, but it is understood from the fact that the recipients are poor and needy.[4] Thus, life in the kingdom is characterized by giving without expecting a return. This redistribution to the needy is the practical implementation of the divine reversal.

This emphasis upon the nonexpectance of a return is balanced, however, by a promise of return and generous rewards from God. Many exhortations to give without expecting a return conclude with a promise of reward, for instance, in the form of repayment at the resurrection or of a treasure in heaven (6:35; 12:33; 14:14). So in this model of exchange there are three parties involved. First, there is a human patron or benefactor. He or she is supposed to give to the second party, one of the needy, without expecting a return. The human benefactor is repaid, however, by a third party, God, who is the great benefactor. In the admonitions to give, the promise of a reward from God serves as a motivation for human patrons to give without expecting a return. In this way, God is the protector and the benefactor of the poor and the needy.

When we turn to passages addressing the recipients of gifts, we notice a great emphasis on the need to *trust* the system of redistribution, for instance, in 11:9–11: "Ask and it will be given to you. . . . For everyone who asks receives." The imperative "ask," however, is without human addressees. Moreover, the passive form of *dothēsetai* ("it will be given") indicates that it is God who will respond to their requests.[5] Likewise, in the exhortation not to worry about food and clothes, it is God who is the source of everything that the faithful need for their subsistence (12:29–31; 18:29–30). The simile in 11:11–13 is a good illustration of the kind of patron–client or benefactor–recipient relationship that Luke has in mind. Luke applies this example of the basic trust that a son can have in his father by a "how much more" analogy to the trust that a believer can have in God.

Nowhere, however, are the needy urged to trust the rich. On the one hand, those who have resources are urged to give to the needy, but without expecting a return; God will see to the reward. On the

4. 6:38; 12:33; 18:22; 19:8.

5. J. Fitzmyer, *Luke (XX–XXIV)*, 915.

other hand, the needy are urged not to trust the wealthy to give them what they need, but God who is the source of all gifts, as well as the daily necessities for human subsistence.

What is the outcome of this form for exchange in terms of social relations? *To give without expecting a return means to interact in such a way as not to make the recipients one's clients!* If one is supposed to act as a patron or benefactor, but without any expectations of gratitude, that takes the power aspect away from the relationship. Patron–client relations were held together by reciprocity within a structure of great inequality in terms of resources and power. In Luke's "economy of the kingdom," human beings cannot play the role of a patron in its traditional form. Instead, they are asked to give gifts without restrictions, to redistribute without making the recipients their clients. Similarly, the recipients are not bound in gratitude or loyalty to the wealthy who give them gifts. God is the only patron; consequently, all people are his clients. And God will give rewards and repay the wealthy for their gifts to others.

Thus, this model of economic interaction has important consequences for social relations. It is a form of giving which makes other people free. It does not bind in servitude or gratitude to other people. All gratitude is to be directed towards God. It is here that we find a definite break with the system of reciprocity found in classical antiquity. There are many similarities between Luke's Gospel and Homer's *Odyssey* in terms of the structural function of generosity. Generosity (but not primarily towards the poor) was also regarded a virtue in Hellenistic times. An integral part of that generosity, however, was the reward through praise and honor.[6] Likewise, in traditional peasant societies, generosity is transformed into prestige and power.[7] It is this social mechanism that is completely undercut in "the economy of the kingdom" in Luke's Gospel.

This is no small matter, but linked to the very center of the message of Jesus. Luke shows the importance of this aspect by introducing it in his version of the Last Supper. In his redaction,

6. See above, p. 133.

7. M. Sahlins, *Stone Age Economics,* 204–8.

the farewell meal also includes a discussion of the role of the Twelve, as well as Jesus' testament to them. The discussion of who is greatest takes a central part, and it is here that Jesus compares them to contemporary rulers: "The kings of the Gentiles exercise lordship over them; and those in authority over them are called benefactors. But not so with you; rather let the greatest among you become as the youngest, and the leader as one who serves" (22:25–26). Claims to be benefactors with the right to rule over others are contrasted with the role of the disciples. The system of power and status in society is taken for granted, both on a larger, political level and in the household: "For which is the greater, one who sits at table, or one who serves? Is it not the one who sits at table?" (22:27). But then Jesus enters the picture: "But I am among you as one who serves."

This introduces a status reversal and a new concept of leadership and benefaction. Luke has emphasized the power and authority of Jesus in his conflict with Jewish leaders, a conflict that ended by their being utterly discredited as leaders. But neither Jesus nor the disciples are merely replacing the Pharisees and other Jewish leaders in their traditional roles. A normal alternative to "bad leaders" would be "good leaders," who used their power to the benefit of their clients. This would be the sign of true benefactors who could legitimately claim honor and respect from their clients. Luke's model is different in that it breaks with the patron–client relationship. Even the good benefactor shall not lay claim to the title "big man";[8] patronage shall not be used to create clients and to create a power base of followers.

The Twelve are installed as rulers and judges over Israel (22:29–30), but at the same time they are to imitate Jesus in the role of the servant. They are asked to perform a function of benefaction without claiming power for themselves, and without distinguishing themselves above others. Greatness is not to be transformed into privilege and power.

So a form of leadership is accepted, but strong checks and balances are introduced. Metaphors like "children" and "servants"

8. The term "big man" is used by Sahlins in his study of Melanesian leaders, *Stone Age Economics,* 135–39, 248–54.

used of believers and community leaders represent an egalitarian tendency with a criticism of patrons and haughty leaders.[9] In the context of Luke's picture of Palestinian society at the time of Jesus, this alternative represents a return to a simpler form for social organization, based on the solidarity of the village community and upon a rejection of the patronage system controlled by the rich elite. This is the result if we read Luke's Gospel at the surface level of the story about Jesus in his time.

ECONOMY IN THE GOSPEL AND IN ACTS: TWO PERSPECTIVES

So far we have concentrated primarily upon Luke's discussion of economy within the Gospel narrative, with occasional references to Acts. In our attempt to relate Luke's views to a possible social setting for him and his community, we need to make a closer comparison between the Gospel and Acts. There seem to be real differences between the Gospel and Acts in several areas. For instance, the Pharisees are viewed more favorably in Acts than in the Gospel. Economy is likewise an area that seems to have another function in Acts than in the Gospel.

A major theme in Luke's Gospel is the coming of Jesus to preach the gospel to the poor (4:18). Jesus has come as the benefactor to the people of Israel. Both the Old Testament and the Hellenistic background of Luke contribute to making socioeconomic relationships among the Jewish people a focusing point. The goal of Jesus' proclamation was to reestablish Israel as the people of God. An alternative structure of social and economic relations was part of salvation.

In Acts, the narrative structure is different. The basic structural outline is provided by the mission from Jerusalem to Rome. Its main message is the proclamation of Jesus as the risen Christ.[10] Consequently, the apostles are above all "witnesses to the resurrection of Jesus."[11] Acceptance or rejection of the resurrection of Jesus marks the dividing line between followers and sympathizers on the one hand, and enemies and opponents on the other. Since

9. Cf. 9:46–48; 12:35–48; 17:7–10; 18:15–17.
10. Acts 2:22–36; 3:17–26; 4:8–12; 5:28–32; etc.
11. 1:22; 2:32; 3:15; 4:33; etc.

the Pharisees believed in the resurrection of the dead, they are described as sympathizers and they come down on the positive side of the dividing line. The Sadducees, however, who did not believe in resurrection, are squarely placed on the negative side (23:6–10; 26:5–8).

In Luke's Gospel, the Pharisees are portrayed in light of the conflict over social relations within Israel. The description of the Pharisees followed a well-known pattern of criticism of opponents and leaders for avarice and greed. A similar criticism is found in Acts (8:18–24; 19:23–41), but now not directed at the Pharisees. Therefore, it seems to be a motif that is not necessarily linked to the Pharisees, but attached to any opponent.

Questions about money and economic and social relations play different roles in the Gospel and in Acts respectively. In the Gospel, they are of structural significance, so that a study of "money" takes us to the very center of the Gospel message. In Acts, it is more of a "supporting" theme, not a key to the whole story.

It is only in the Gospel that we find the reversal theme, the promise that God will reverse the fortunes of the rich and the poor in his intervention to create justice in Israel (1:51–53; 6:20–26; 16:19–26). Jesus' proclamation of the good news to the poor parallels his inclusion of the outcasts in Israel, like tax collectors and sinners, and gives the Gospel its characteristic emphasis upon "hospitality to outsiders" and the bringing-in of the outcasts.

In Acts, the situation changes from one of a conflict within Palestine to one of contrasts between groups of believers in Christ and the society that surrounds them. Thus, in the first chapters of Acts the believers in Jerusalem are described as an ideal community, one of whose main characteristics is redistribution of resources to members in need (2:43–47; 4:32–37; 5:1–11). This part of Acts sums up a pattern of the system of "moral economy" that prevailed in the Gospel. However, as the Christian mission spreads to Asia, Greece, and Rome, the notion of the reestablishment of Israel as a pattern of "moral" social and economic relations disappears from Luke's narrative. The same is true of the emphasis on the inclusion of the poor together with the unclean and outcasts.

Even motifs common to the Gospel and to Acts receive different emphasis. Almsgiving is a Lukan theme, both in Acts and in the Gospel, and it is a theme that most likely was introduced to his material by Luke. It is only in the Gospel, however, that almsgiving is of structural importance, describing a social and economic relationship. In Acts, the function of almsgiving is different; together with prayer, it serves as part of a pattern of characteristics belonging to the righteous man (10:2, 31).

The leaders of the church in Acts—Peter, John (3:6), and Paul (20:33–35)—are not "lovers of money." They conform to the Greek ideal of good teachers who do not have money and who work for their living. The opponents of the apostles in Acts are greedy and avaricious, just as were the opponents of Jesus in the Gospel. But here, too, it is more a matter of a description of negative personal characteristics than of social relations. This time, the main opponents are competitors to the apostles.[12] Thus, in Acts too, resistance to the good news is accompanied by avarice, but it is more in terms of a "code word" than as an explained pattern of interaction.

In sum, there are many similarities between Acts and Luke's Gospel in the area of economy: women serve as patrons (Luke 8:1–3; Acts 9:36–43); almsgiving is necessary so that people's needs shall be met; avarice and greed are negative characteristics. These are typically Lukan features, and we therefore can expect them to come out of and be a response to his milieu. On the other hand, it is only in the Gospel that social and economic relations are central to the plot of Luke's narrative. Moreover, it is only in the Gospel that Luke develops a system of social and economic relations that we have called the "economy of the kingdom," in contrast to that of the "old order" under oppressive rulers and bad leaders.

In Acts, the narrative highlights how the message spread from Jerusalem to Rome. Reflective, perhaps, of this move, the narrative also moves away from a message embedded in a social situation, aimed at the totality of Israel, to become a message for small groups, with no aims of restructuring society as such, but

12. Simon Magus, 8:18–24; the silversmiths of Artemis in Ephesus, 19:23–41.

content to establish an alternative structure among a community of believers.

What does this tell us about Luke's own position and about his community?

LUKE AND HIS COMMUNITY

We have focused on social and economic relations in the world described by Luke. It is Luke's portrayal of the Pharisees and the structure of village life in Palestine that has been our main concern.

But what is the point of contact between that picture of Palestine and Luke's message to his readers? Why did Luke write the way he did? It is helpful to see Luke within the tradition of history writing of his time. There was no conflict between the ideal of a true historical rendering of the past and telling the story with the purpose of influencing one's readers.[13] In this way, Luke's narrative becomes transparent, so that it is made relevant for his readers.

Thus, Luke describes the world of Jesus in Palestine, but in such a way that his readers would recognize it. It was partly an unfamiliar world, but partly also a familiar one. Luke's redactional comments served to make this world more relevant and familiar. As we have noticed, *almsgiving* and *criticism of self-righteousness* were elements that served to structure his narrative and to elucidate his main points.

Redaction criticism studies the Gospels primarily as statements addressed to Christian communities at the time of the evangelists. This is an important and relevant perspective. In this study, however, the main emphasis has been upon the way in which Luke tells his story. From the portrait that emerges from such a study one can proceed to the next step, an investigation of Luke's advice to his community as well as to the historical question of the social composition of his audience. To a brief discussion of that question we now turn.

Both the teaching about "poor and rich" and the portrait of the Pharisees have been analyzed with a view to the identity of Luke's

13. D. E. Aune, *New Testament and Its Literary Environment,* 77–115.

community in terms of social composition and internal relations.[14] Some scholars have identified the "rich Pharisees" with rich members of Luke's community.[15] It has also been argued that rather than speaking to the poor, Luke speaks to the rich and addresses their concerns about the danger of money.[16]

There are many difficulties involved, however, when one tries to conclude from a narrative the historical situation to which the narrative was first addressed. In many instances, Luke talks about a historical situation that may be very different from that of his readers. Moreover, literary structure and narrative patterns do not necessarily reflect or speak to a community situation; they may be part of narrative conventions.[17]

Since the Pharisees are characterized as rich persons who rejected Jesus, it is unlikely that Luke intended them to be "types" of rich Christians. It makes more sense to think of them as negative representations of outsiders to the community.[18] The similarities between the portrait of the Pharisees in Luke's Gospel and the polemic against false teachers in the pastoral letters[19] suggest that Luke has created negative figures as an antithesis to his paraenesis. Therefore, "the rich" are not necessarily figures to be identified as "a type" for members of the community he is addressing.[20] The literary construct of the rich Pharisee might function as an exaggerated picture of the nonbelieving world, in a fashion similar to the vice lists in paraenetical literature.

Instead of trying to identify members of Luke's community behind figures in the Gospel, it seems better to focus on the

14. For an overview, see R. J. Karris, "Poor and Rich: The Lukan Sitz im Leben," in *Perspectives on Luke-Acts*, ed. C. H. Talbert (Danville: Association of Baptist Professors of Religion, 1978), 112–25.

15. Karris, "Poor and Rich," passim; F. W. Horn, *Glaube und Handeln in der Theologie des Lukas* (Göttingen, W. Ger.: Vandenhoeck & Ruprecht, 1983), 225.

16. Karris, "Poor and Rich," 124.

17. See Luke T. Johnson, "On Finding the Lukan Community: A Cautious Cautionary Essay," *SBLSP* (1979): 87–100.

18. C. Osiek, *Rich and Poor in the Shepherd of Hermas*, CBQMS 15 (Washington, D.C.: Catholic Biblical Association of America, 1983), 29–32.

19. See above, pp. 6–8.

20. See Luke T. Johnson, "1–2 Timothy and the Polemic against False Teachers: A Re-examination," *JRelS* 6/2 and 7/1 (1978–79): 4.

structures of the social and economic relations that Luke describes. What clues can they give to the social composition of Luke's audience? We noticed the attempt to identify the "rich" in the Gospel with well-to-do members of Luke's community. The results of our study of social relations in the Gospel narrative appear to point in a different direction.

First, in most of the Gospel narratives, "the rich" are negative figures. Second, Luke's criticism was based on what we called "the moral economy of the peasant." At this point it is necessary to consider who the "rich" were in the kind of society that Luke describes. The rich were not just persons with much wealth; they also belonged to the urban elite, very distant from the ordinary peasant villagers and their needs.[21] A "rich" person in the Gospel narratives is a person with power and influence. Status was more important than money. The elites were rich, but wealth did not automatically give access to elite status. Freedmen or "resident aliens" like merchants might be rich, but did not belong to the elite. For instance, the tax collector Zacchaeus (Luke 19:1–10) was rich in the sense that he had much money, but he did not belong to the elite. Rather, he was an outsider.

"Rich" and "poor" are, therefore, imprecise categories to describe Luke's community. They apply more to some industrialized societies in which economic distinctions take precedence over birth and status. A better set of categories for the first-century Mediterranean world is "elite" and "nonelite." The elite, who were rich, made up only a tiny percentage of the population and resided in the cities. The nonelite were the great bulk of the population, maybe as much as ninety-five to ninety-eight percent. The vast majority of the nonelite were peasants; in addition were the lower-status urban dwellers. Among the urban nonelite were merchants, artisans, lower clergy, skilled and unskilled workers, and the poor.

The major differences were to be found between the elite and the nonelite, not between the urban nonelite and the peasants. The latter groups shared many traits: they both lacked power and therefore were dependent upon the elite. A mode of thinking characterized as "the moral economy of the peasant," with its

21. Cf. for the following G. Sjøberg, *Preindustrial City,* 108–44.

emphasis on the need for subsistence, would therefore apply to the urban nonelite as well. Even the more well-to-do among them were in an insecure position, due to their lack of power.

Against this background, it is difficult to imagine that Luke would have used "rich" to characterize members of his community, even to admonish them. The positive structure of social relations identified with almsgiving is not primarily associated with the rich, but rather with followers and disciples (cf. 6:27; 12:33). We should not imagine Luke's community as a group with enormous disparity between some members who belonged to the rich elite and some who belonged to the city poor. It is more likely that most members belonged to the same nonelite class. There still would be differences between them regarding wealth and possessions, and therefore the need for support in the form of almsgiving, but not in terms of a contrast between social elite and nonelite.[22]

The existing inequalities, however, could be a source of tension. Luke's advice to give without expecting a return speaks to the dangers of creating patron–client relations within the community. Contrary to Hellenistic expectations, those who gave alms or rendered loans were expected to forgo not only returns in kind, but also in the form of gratitude, status, and recognition. They were urged to behave as benefactors, but without any of the social remunerations normally awarded benefactors. This speaks against the suggestions that Luke addresses the rich and also argues from the perspective of the rich.

As an educated person, Luke himself must have had some social status and some means. But that does not mean that he belonged to the rich elite. Furthermore, he does not speak from their perspective, nor does he support the ambitions of the affluent nonelite who might want to become patrons of the community. His admonitions to give are based on the need for subsistence for those with few resources. Moreover, his emphasis upon a "nonreturn" represents a pressure from a perspective "from below." The lowly and needy are not to be put in a dependent position. In this way, Luke argued for a community structure that undercut the very basis for patron–client relations.

22. This is similar to the suggestion regarding Hermas's community by Osiek, *Rich and Poor in the Shepherd of Hermas*, 134–35.

THE CHALLENGE: TO SEE THE WORLD "FROM THE VIEWPOINT OF THE POOR"

In this study we have used models from social and economic anthropology to identify types of social interaction and economic exchange. Thus, we were able to view more clearly the alternative to the social structure that Luke criticized, an alternative that we termed "the economy of the kingdom."

But where did this model for economic and social exchange originate? For the "new" model is not merely another version of "peasant economics" with a just and fair patron–client system; rather, we noticed a break with the system itself and a departure from the patron–client structure of society. There was a strong impulse among the first Christians, visible not only in Luke's description of economic exchange but also in Paul's ideal of equality within the community, couched in honor-shame categories.[23] This impulse went contrary to known social forces, as well as forces within a "peasant economy" that was instinctively conservative. There is a newness to this ideal that points to an original source and to the very beginning of a movement. It points toward the influence of Jesus and his unique function as initiator and leader of a new movement. Therefore, using models for the study of social groups and economic relations has brought us to the point where we encounter a genuinely theological question: that of the role of Jesus, not only as starter of a movement, but as a continuous source of inspiration, challenge, and salvation.

Seeing Luke's sayings about money as models for social relations and interactions also brings another insight. These are not words addressed to the individual about attitudes toward possessions and one's own salvation. Rather, Luke addresses social and economic relations in Palestinian society in their totality. His "economic" advice is not merely addressed to the individual; he is concerned with the total structure of relations between people in terms of power, rights, and resources.

Traditionally, many churches and Christians have regarded the question of money and wealth as a matter for the individual. Admonitions to "give," not to be avaricious, and others have been

23. H. Moxnes, "Honor and Righteousness in Romans," *JSNT* 32 (1988): 61–77.

addressed to the individual. This often has left economic structures, policies of large corporations, and national politics that create economic and social inequalities unaffected. Luke strongly urges his audience to see the role of the individual within a context of social relations. Moreover, he points out that money and economic systems are not neutral. Rather, "mammon" is an economic system of exploitation and profit. When "money" becomes an end in itself, and not a means to be used for common needs, it becomes demonic and a threat to human coexistence. Mammon instead of God is the perennial threat, and it comes in such alluring disguises: production, progress, prosperity—but only for some. It forms the perspectives and the politics of present-day elites.

This is a perspective that it is difficult to change. Still, there are efforts made to develop alternatives both within and outside of Christian churches.[24] One recent example is the United States Catholic bishops' pastoral letter on Catholic social teaching and the United States economy, *Economic Justice for All.*[25] Its emphasis is upon the communal responsibilities of economic life. From within a long tradition of Catholic social teaching, it expresses the concerns of a "moral economy": "The fundamental moral criterion for all economic decisions, policies and institutions is this: They must be at the service of all people, especially the poor" (12). One of the moral priorities of the nation is "to make a fundamental 'option for the poor.' The obligation to evaluate social and economic activity from the viewpoint of the poor and the powerless arises from the radical command to love one's neighbor as one's self" (45).

The bishops' letter is a strong and passionate document, well informed about the workings of the economy in the United States. So why read Luke, who comes out of a totally different social and economic system, one which is hardly relevant to today's marketplace?[26] One phrase in the quotation from the letter catches the

24. For the attention paid to this question in the World Council of Churches, see P. Bock, *In Search of a Responsible World Society: The Social Teaching of the World Council of Churches* (Philadelphia: Westminster Press, 1974), 52–88, 186–224.

25. Washington: National Conference of Catholic Bishops, 1986.

26. Cf. Bruce J. Malina's criticism that the biblical perspective of "poor" is totally different from that of the bishops' letter, "Interpreting the Bible with Anthropology: The Case of the Poor and the Rich," *Listening* 21 (1986): 148–59.

eye: "The obligation to evaluate social and economic activity from the viewpoint of the poor and the powerless." How can those who are at least relatively affluent evaluate from the viewpoint of the poor and the powerless? If this is a moral obligation for Christians, how can it be carried out?

Maybe this is where Luke comes in, his Gospel read not as a moral exhortation but as a narrative with all the powers and enchantments of a story. A common feature in Luke's stories is the appearance of "the other": the woman, the poor person, the stranger who suddenly takes center stage. Those who are in control of social rules, of space, and of possessions are dispossessed; their world is turned upside down. Not the rich, but the poor are close to God (16:19–31), not the morally superior, but the impure have their life from the love of God (7:36–50). For the elites, this is a fatal "de-centering of perspective."[27] These narratives serve as preparations for the final judgment, when God will cast the rich from their thrones (1:52–53) and cause the reversal of the fates of the rich and the poor (6:20–26). In the company of Jesus and in his parables, "the other"—the stranger, the outcast, the needy person—comes into the lives of the elites, those in command, those who are confident of their identity. The point of the parables and of the narratives is not merely "moral behavior," but also a "de-centering of perspective" and a reversal of the world as it is presently known and legitimized. The poor and the needy come into this world not as mere recipients of gifts from the wealthy, but as those upon whom the future of the world is dependent. A "sinful woman," a tax collector, and an outsider represent the signs of "the economy of the kingdom."

How can the affluent evaluate social and economic activity in our world from the viewpoint of the poor and the powerless? The uncomfortable truth is that we cannot. Only the poor and the powerless can do that. Thus, the only hope for a reversal comes from their being empowered to act on their insights. It is when we

27. A phrase from Paul Ricoeur, *Freedom and Nature: The Voluntary and the Involuntary* (Evanston, Ill.: Northwestern University Press, 1966), 126; quoted in Thomas W. Ogletree's *Hospitality to the Stranger: Dimensions of Moral Understanding* (Philadelphia: Fortress Press, 1985), 2. Ogletree's book has inspired many of the following reflections.

recognize the force of "the moral economy" of black women in the United States, of miners in South Africa, or of Indian peasants in Latin America, to name only a few examples, that we really understand the force of Luke's narratives.

It is relatively easy to read the narratives as exhortations to benevolence and generosity towards the poor. This is a reading that can give instant gratification to the affluent. It is much more difficult to read them as stories empowering the poor, bringing liberation from the bonds of ideological dependency upon the wealthy. Both in the community described by Luke and in today's society, the structures of domination and exploitation by the powerful are in place, but the Gospel offers a liberation from the world view that legitimizes them.

Just as Luke shatters some stereotypes, he reinforces others! The Gospel presentations of the Pharisees have for centuries enforced stereotypes about Jews, turning them into "the others." The long and sometimes disastrous history of Jews suffering at the hands of Christian majorities is a proof of that. But in the same manner as the stereotyped Pharisees of the Gospel were confronted with the human in the impure, the poor, and the outcast, our stereotypical characterizations of the Jews must be corrected through human encounters and exchanges. Historical scholarship has shown that the New Testament authors have a much too negative, sometimes outright false, picture of the Pharisees and of the Jews in general. It is understandable, considering the conflicts at the time of writing. But it is inexcusable to continue to spread this false portrayal as if it were a historical truth. The message of the Gospel forces us to give up that very portrait of the Pharisees that Luke created! In recent years, Jewish-Christian dialogues have alerted Christians to the need for self-criticism and change in our relations to Jews.

This issue also concerns our attitudes to all people, especially those who are foreign to us, "the others," who seem strange and reprehensible. As individuals, classes, and nations, we tend to divide people into friends, similar to ourselves, and the others, strangers, possible threats to us. This is a way to close ourselves off from other people and also to deny the love of God towards all people. To break these divisions—mentally, socially, and economically—is the real challenge to our individual and communal lives.

Suggestions for Further Reading

HISTORICAL AND BIBLICAL STUDIES

Finley, Moses I. *The Ancient Economy.* Berkeley and Los Angeles: University of California Press, 1973. An excellent introduction to the economy of the ancient world within its political, social, and cultural framework.

Finley, Moses I. *The World of Odysseus.* New York: Viking Press, 1965. A book that served as a model for our study. Basing his study on a reading of the text and upon anthropological studies of other societies, Finley renders a fascinating portrait of the society envisaged in the *Odyssey.*

Freyne, Seán. *Galilee from Alexander the Great to Hadrian, 323 B.C.E. to 135 C.E.* Wilmington: Michael Glazier, 1980. A very comprehensive study of Galilee, its geography and political history, as well as its social, cultural, and religious situation. An excellent companion to the Gospel narratives about Jesus in Galilee.

Hands, A. R. *Charities and Social Aid in Greece and Rome.* London: Thames & Hudson, 1968. A very fine study of Greco-Roman views of poverty and charity, providing an interesting background and contrast to the views of Jesus and the New Testament authors.

Neusner, Jacob. *From Politics to Piety: The Emergence of Pharisaic Judaism.* Englewood Cliffs, N.J.: Prentice-Hall, 1979. A summary of Neusner's authoritative works on the Pharisees. Written from a historical-critical perspective, this book provides the best introduction to the question of who the Pharisees were.

Ogletree, Thomas W. *Hospitality to the Stranger.* Philadelphia: Fortress Press, 1985. Based on biblical images, this is a challenge to make the encounter with "the stranger" the starting point for ethical reflection. Especially valuable is a discussion of how to define "needs" and "values."

Ringe, Sharon H. *Jesus, Liberation, and the Biblical Jubilee.* Philadelphia: Fortress Press, 1985. Excellent study of the "Jubilee" in biblical thought and how its images influence our understanding of Jesus' proclamation.

Rivkin, E. *A Hidden Revolution.* Nashville: Abingdon Press, 1978. An alternative to the consensual definition of the Pharisees as a sect concerned with purity. Rivkin argues vigorously that they were politically active, a class of revolutionaries.

LUKAN STUDIES

Bailey, K. E. *Poet and Peasant: A Literary-Cultural Approach to the Parables in Luke.* Grand Rapids: Wm. B. Eerdmans, 1976. Stimulating reading of the parables, based upon personal knowledge of Middle Eastern cultures more than upon systematic use of models.

Horn, F. W. *Glaube und Handeln in der Theologie des Lukas.* Göttingen, W. Ger.: Vandenhoeck & Ruprecht, 1983. A technical study, but highly rewarding reading. It treats "economic" behavior within a comprehensive framework of Luke's ethics.

Johnson, Luke T. *The Literary Function of Possessions in Luke-Acts.* SBLDS 39. Missoula, Mont.: Scholars Press, 1977. Scholarly study arguing convincingly that money has a symbolic function in Luke, linked to the acceptance or rejection of Jesus.

Pilgrim, W. *Good News to the Poor: Wealth and Poverty in Luke-Acts.* Minneapolis: Augsburg Publishing House, 1981. A good starting point, it provides a summary of many recent studies in the area and gives a discussion of all the pertinent passages.

SOCIAL SCIENCE STUDIES AND SOCIAL-SCIENTIFIC APPROACHES TO THE NEW TESTAMENT

Carney, T. F. *The Shape of the Past: Models and Antiquity.* Lawrence, Kans.: Coronado Press, 1975. A stimulating introduction to the study of ancient societies, presenting models that are appropriate to understand them.

Elliott, John H. *A Home for the Homeless: A Sociological Exegesis of 1 Peter, Its Situation and Strategy.* Philadelphia: Fortress Press, 1981. Discusses important presuppositions of social-scientific analysis and the literature through 1980. It was the first systematic application of this analysis to a specific biblical book.

Eisenstadt, S. N., and L. Roniger. *Patrons, Clients, and Friends.* Cambridge: Cambridge University Press, 1984. Sometimes hard to read, but a valuable historical and systematic study of patron–client relations and friendship as social institutions, and of their role in various societies.

Malina, Bruce J. *The New Testament World: Insights from Cultural Anthropology.* Atlanta: John Knox Press, 1981. Malina uses anthropology to open up a fascinating new world in reading the New Testament, bringing to the fore many of the culturally presupposed values that lie behind biblical narratives.

Malina, Bruce J. *Christian Origins and Cultural Anthropology.* Atlanta: John Knox Press, 1986. More demanding than the other book, it puts emphasis on models from cultural anthropology to bring about a double process of interpretation, of our own cultures and of that of the Bible.

Pitt-Rivers, J. A. *The People of the Sierra.* 2d ed. Chicago: University of Chicago Press, 1971. A classical study which gives a fascinating picture of life, social relations, and values in a small town in Andalusia, Spain.

"Social-Scientific Criticism of the New Testament and Its Social World," *Semeia* 35 (1986), ed. John H. Elliott. This issue of *Semeia*, a journal dedicated to experimental Bible study, provides a theoretical discussion of the use of social-scientific methods as well as several essays applying such methods to New Testament passages, by, among others, John H. Elliott, Bruce J. Malina, and Jerome H. Neyrey.

Sahlins, M. *Stone Age Economics.* Chicago: Aldine Publishing, 1972. An influential study of the economic patterns of "primitive" societies, especially good in its descriptions of various forms of reciprocities and their social location.

Scott, James C. *The Moral Economy of the Peasant: Rebellion and Subsistence in Southeast Asia.* New Haven: Yale University Press, 1976. An important book for understanding the values and norms of peasant societies. Scott places the concern for subsistence at the center of his study of peasant behavior in the face of outside exploitation in Southeast Asia.

Glossary of Anthropological and Economic Terms

BROKER. Mediator or middleman between two parties of society, or between individuals: for instance, between the urban elite and peasant society, or between a large landowner and a village community. Pp. 44, 59–60, 63–64, 73–74.

CONSPICUOUS CONSUMPTION. A consumption not based on *need*, but on a desire to show off in order to preserve or to enhance status and power, for instance, by means of big feasts. Pp. 31, 88–90, 130–31.

ECONOMY, EMBEDDED. Ancient economy was not a separate sector of society, but one of several actions performed by the social and political institutions (for instance, household, temple, ruler) of a society. Pp. 27–32.

ECONOMY, MORAL. Term used of the economic values of underprivileged groups. "The moral economy of the peasants" is the peasants' notion of economic justice and of exploitation; its central value is the household's need for subsistence. Pp. 32, 79–83, 93–97.

FAMILY OR HOUSEHOLD. The primary social unit, based on kinship and/or cohabitation. Its main activities are production for need and consumption. Pp. 33–34, 61.

FRIENDSHIP. Formalized relationship between two individuals, based on equality with moral obligations. Pp. 43, 62, 70, 142.

LIMITED GOOD. A notion found in peasant economy (according to G. Foster) that all resources are in limited supply, resulting in a defensive attitude in order to preserve one's resources. Pp. 76–79.

MARKET EXCHANGE. Economic transactions that are not governed by the social relations between the individuals engaged in this exchange; thus, market exchange is possible between strangers or members of different ethnic groups. Pp. 64–66.

PATRON–CLIENT RELATIONSHIP. Relations between two parties (individuals) characterized by inequality and asymmetry in power and status, combined with mutual solidarity and obligations: for example, landlord–tenant, ruler–servants. Pp. 40–47.

POOR. People who belong to the nonelite, and who in addition to physical need also suffer social deprivation and loss of status. Pp. 58, 103, 117, 167–69.

RECIPROCITY. Economic exchange between two parties that have different socioeconomic interests. This exchange takes different forms: (1) Generalized reciprocity indicates altruistic transactions; ideal is the "pure gift." (2) Balanced reciprocity represents an attempt to reach equivalence in goods and services. (3) Negative reciprocity is an attempt to get something for nothing, if necessary with force. Pp. 34–35, 129–34.

REDISTRIBUTION. Economic exchange within a group. Resources are collected by a central authority and redistributed, either directly (for instance, to clients, to the poor) or indirectly, to serve collective interests (for instance, warfare, temple liturgies). Pp. 35, 38–40.

RICH. Not a mere "economic" term in a modern sense, but designating people who belong to the (urban) elite, of high status accompanied by power and great wealth. Pp. 57, 89, 92, 164.

SUBSISTENCE. What is needed for a household to be a fully functioning member of a village society. It includes food, clothes, housing, but also resources to cover social and ceremonial obligations, for instance, for hospitality, tithes, and offerings. Pp. 80–82.

VILLAGE. A peasant settlement that functions as a self-sufficient community and as a geographical, social, and cultural unit. Pp. 50–51.

Index of Ancient Sources

Old Testament

New Testament

Other Ancient Texts

Index of Modern Authors